the
SHARECROPPER'S
SON

Al Martin

INTRODUCTION

This book started out with the intention of just making a few notes about my childhood on the farm, so that my children and grandchildren would know how life on the farm was in the "old days". None of them grew up in the country, and certainly not on a farm, so their early life was completely different from mine. As I continued to make notes, I began to think that others might like to read about another lifestyle unlike their own. My note taking started about twenty years ago. The book started about ten years ago. I became serious about two years ago. I'm now 82 years old. Maybe I'll finish in the current decade of my life.

Life on our farm was different from many others back then, since we farmed in an old fashioned way, using horses instead of tractors. Some other farmers used horses, but most used modern equipment. Our way meant farming was more labor intensive and it took longer to plow a field, harvest a crop or most anything we had to do. This is the way my father, the Sharecropper, continued to farm the rest of his life.

The early part of this story took place in the era of The Great Depression. It's a story of heartache, hard work, and finally, accomplishment by The Sharecropper, my father.

I thank you for reading this far and hope you will continue and enjoy my stories about life on the farm.

DEDICATION

To my family and other sharecroppers' sons

Illustration by Hannah Rose Meyer

The Sharecropper's Son

©2020 Al Martin

print ISBN: 978-1-09834-875-5

ebook ISBN: 978-1-09834-876-2

CONTENTS

Chapter 1:

THE VOYAGE OF
THE SHARECROPPER

His life's journey began June 29, 1892 on his father's farm in the rolling foothills of the Blue Ridge Mountains in Patrick County, Virginia. He was the ninth of sixteen children born to William Wingfield (Billy Buck) Martin and Louise Elizabeth (Betty) Ayers Martin. Billy Buck was a tough, no-nonsense, stern man who had always been independent. In addition to raising children, the family patriarch grew tobacco, corn, wheat, apples, peaches, and lots of vegetables to feed his children. Billy Buck, born in 1854 to Berryman Jennings Martin and Susan Edwards Martin, was the picture of health and lived near age ninety-five when he died in his sleep. He was tall and slim, had a white beard to match his white, always-tangled hair, and was grim-looking. In pictures, he never smiled and seemed tired of this picture taking and wanted to get on with something else. Grandma Betty was standing beside her man with a sweet smile, like Whistler's Mother. She was kind to everyone, even after raising sixteen children and having around eighty grandchildren. Because they lived in Patrick County and we lived in Amelia, and transportation was near non-existent for us, I only saw them two or three times and was too young to understand that I was in the presence of history. Grandpa was born before the Civil War, and Grandma was born the year it started; we could have had some great talks if I had been interested, but I was too young. By the time I might have been interested, they had passed, he in 1949 and she 1951, while I was too young to appreciate history of any kind.

My father, George Ruffin (Ruff) Martin, who would become the sharecropper, was born in sight of his father's tobacco field, and never strayed far from his roots or from the roots of the tobacco plant that his father grew. His family lived in a two-story white house on the side of a hill overlooking the good bottom land where many of their crops were grown. He was born in the middle of the sixteen children. I expect the older siblings helped raise him and the other young ones, as was the custom at that time. His turn to help came later, as the family grew. No one left the family until they were ready to start one of their own. His father was a good man and loved his children; his word was law, and he knew what was best for the family. When "Ruff" was age twenty-eight, the time came for him to leave his family and the security he had always known. He joined some of his older siblings, and some other Patrick County people, who had moved to Amelia County to start their families and better their lives in an area that would come to be known as "Little Patrick." It was hard for him to leave the rolling foothills of Patrick County that he knew so well, his father and mother, and younger siblings, but it was time to be on his own. He would soon marry the girl that he loved, from the adjoining Carroll County. She had recently moved to Amelia with her father and stepmother.

He and his new bride, Rosie May Burcham (my mother), bought a small farm in Amelia, along with a log house, and started raising their own tobacco. He was determined to make a go of it, if for no other reason than to impress his dad back in Patrick. Their first child, George William, came along in 1921, after their 1920 marriage. "Ruff" was raising tobacco, just like his dad had always done. The 1920s were hard times and money was scarce. After a few years trying to make a go of it, he came to the decision that this farm was not to be; he just didn't have the $500 he needed to pay his mortgage, so he had to move on. He had his pride and would always take care of his family but would have to do it elsewhere. He put his dream of owning his own farm on hold and became a sharecropper.

Sharecropping, especially at that time, was common in the South, and many former slaves, as well as many others who didn't have the money to purchase their own land, were sharecroppers. Sharecropping was a way for the tenant farmer to make a living using someone else's land with an agreement that the harvest would be shared by the landowner and the farmer/sharecropper. There were many different agreements between the sharecroppers and landowners. Some required the landowner to provide the fertilizer and seed and in exchange would receive a larger share of the harvest; others agreed that the sharecropper would take care of that and would get a larger share of the harvest. Sometimes, the landowner may have been unable to work the land, and this would be a good way to still make money without working the land himself. The sharecropper was able to work the land but didn't own land to work, so this was a good deal for both parties to the agreement. However, the landowner was in a position of greater power, so would sometimes take advantage of the sharecropper.

Also, remember, the times that we are speaking of were just before and during the Great Depression, and for most, times were really hard. In the depths of the Depression, many people didn't have jobs. The unemployment rate reached as high as 25%. If people didn't have jobs, they didn't have money to spend and couldn't buy products that businesses had for sale. A catch twenty-two situation. There were essentially no government programs of assistance until President Roosevelt, elected in 1933, actually kept some people from starving with his various programs of support. One such program was the Civilian Conservation Corps started in 1933 and continued until 1942. This was a voluntary public works program which employed young, unmarried men from age eighteen to twenty-five, later expanded to age twenty-eight. They worked on public land such as parks, planting trees, digging ditches, clearing fire trails in forests, and whatever was needed. I vaguely remember men working on fire trails in forests near our home, which allowed for access roads into forests so firefighters could more easily fight fires. This public works program helped the unemployed and served a good public need. Another program was the WPA or Works

Progress Administration, which employed millions of people seeking jobs. The WPA was started in 1935 and eventually supplied jobs for over eight million people in its peak times. It was discontinued in 1943.

After giving up that first farm for lack of money to pay his mortgage, the sharecropper worked several farms but never gave up his dream. He would someday own his own farm and continue to raise bright tobacco, just like his father had done all his life.

His father-in-law, Mac Donald Burcham (my grandpa), who owned a farm but had not worked it since he had started a general store and grain mill, convinced Dad to sharecrop his idle farm. The sharecropper moved his family and took up sharecropping on yet another farm. By this time, his family was complete with six sons and the vivid memory of their beautiful daughter, Betty Ann, who had died of a childhood disease. I was the last child and around age three or four at that time, and this is when my first memories began.

After about three or four years at Grandpa's, Dad picked up his family and moved again, across the county to Mr. Bryant's farm, still sharecropping. This turned out to be a blessing, since it was here that he learned about a nearby property that would make him a farm owner again. The old Eggleston farm, long abandoned, needed a family to move in and make it an active farm again, and I believe it was waiting for us. The sharecropper was so excited he could hardly wait for his crops at Mr. Bryant's to ripen and be harvested so he could make the move. I believe with all my heart that God looked on the Martins with favor for this to happen as it did, in perfect harmony.

The old Eggleston farmhouse was grown over with vines, and the fields were covered with small pine trees that would need to be cleared. Some might have looked at it and thought, "What a mess!" I think the sharecropper looked at it and saw fields of tobacco ripening, wheat and corn fields and a garden of tomatoes ready for eating, beans to be cooked and watermelons ready for slicing, and maybe the old, unkempt house painted gleaming white. He had hit pay dirt. The sharecropper's long journey had ended; although he would be working hard, the payday would be his. He bought his farm and would never be a sharecropper again.

The new farm was purchased in September of 1943 from Mable M. Eggleston, a widow who had lived there several years earlier with her husband, Dr. Eggleston. Much of its 160 acres was covered with timber, which would help to pay off the mortgage of $2,800. Looking at it today, that was certainly the deal of the century. I suspect that it was also a great deal even at the time. The sharecropper, now owner/farmer, worked from before daylight in the mornings to far past dusk. He was going to be successful regardless of any events. He had six years to pay off the mortgage; however, due to some good tobacco crops and by selling timber, he managed to pay it off in three years. He was blessed to have his own farm, free and clear of debt. Even though I was there, I had no idea of this wonderful happening, so I can only imagine the relief and joy Dad and Mom shared.

Many years later after they passed on, I came across some old papers and found the loan application they submitted to the Bank of Powhatan for the $2,800 mortgage. This was approved by Mr. W. R. Parker, bank president who, in Dad's opinion, was a wonderful person because he had made it possible for Dad to have his farm.

In reviewing the deed and mortgage papers, I was interested in the listing of their personal property, which follows:

1. All farm machinery and tools the property G.R. and Rosie B. Martin

2. One bay horse, age 8 years, named "Dan"

3. One brown mare, age 12 years, named "Beauty," and colt

4. Three jersey and Guernsey cows, ages 2, 3, & 7, named "Bloss," "Daisy," and "Hucky"

5. One half jersey and Guernsey cow, age 6, named "Rachael"

6. Two Guernsey color heifers, named "Emma" and "May"

7. One thoroughbred bull, aged 6 months, "Kayo Honey Nobleman"

8. Ninety White Leghorn hens.

9. One hundred White Leghorn Pullets.

My brothers, Bob, Don, and I lived there until we grew up and left home. Bob went to work, Don to college, and I joined the U. S. Navy. Dad and I had a conversation about me staying on the farm and becoming a farmer; however, I only agreed to that if we would modernize operations with a tractor and other up-to-date equipment. I had no desire to follow horses plowing the fields, as he had done all his life. Dad had no interest in making any changes. None of my siblings took up farming, even though George did have a small farm where he raised cattle, not tobacco. The tradition handed down from father to son ended in our family. Even though we left the home place, it was still home to us, and we were always welcomed with open arms. Our parents were happy to see their "boys" come home, especially to have all six sons together as often as possible. I will always remember with joy my boyhood home and family gatherings. Later, Mom and Dad retired from farming and sold the home place. They built a new home and moved up on the "hard-surfaced" road, where we were still welcomed at any time, day or night. However, no place could ever replace the home on the farm where I grew up.

Chapter 2:
THE SHARECROPPER
AND FAMILY

My dad, father of seven children, and my mom, Rosie May, were married for fifty-one years until his death in 1971. Mom was born in 1899 in Morgan County, Illinois, and was one of two children born to MacDonald Burcham and his Cherokee wife, Polly Ann Blackburn. Grandma Polly died soon after the birth of their son, my Uncle Charlie. Mom was a wonderful wife and mother who cared deeply for her family and treated everyone with respect and dignity.

The sharecropper was a man of integrity, honesty, and self-reliance. He believed that a handshake was a contract, not to be broken. The sharecropper had learned these things from his patriarch father who was independent, almost to a fault. They both believed one should take care of their own in every situation. Dad told me about a time when my older siblings were in school and the school sent home a letter saying they would be administering some kind of shot to the children. The cost was $1 and if he could not afford it, it would be free. He told me that he could not afford it but sent the money because he took care of his own children. He also told me of a time when he took a part-time job making $1 per day. Today, with all the welfare programs, he would not like seeing people taking advantage of those programs. It is a different world today. Also, he was a man of faith, although he was not one to discuss how he felt about faith or anything else. He wouldn't even discuss how he voted, which to him was a private matter. Their children: George

William, born in 1921, who had two children; Marion Franklin, born in 1923, who had two children; Marvin Lee, born in 1925, who had no children; Robert, born in 1929, who adopted two children; Betty Ann, born in 1932; Donald Hamner, born in 1935, who had no children; and myself, born in 1937, who had two children. All lived a normal life span, except Betty Ann, who died at twenty months. Dad always said, "The only way one can pay for their own raising is to raise children of their own." They paid their debt.

Everyone who knew my Dad well called him Ruff. I'm reminded of one Christmas when he received a card addressed to Mr. "Rough" Martin. Guess they didn't know him too well. To say that Ruff was a farmer would not say it all. Almost all farmers, especially of that day and time, could do about anything, and did, out of necessity. Money was quite often in limited supply, and things that needed to be repaired were needed immediately, such as harvesting equipment, which simply could not wait for someone to come and repair it. In farming, timing is vital; crops depend on good weather to grow, on natural timing to ripen, and, of course, the farmer's time. He always repaired his equipment, built things, fixed shoes, cut his sons' hair, cut trees, doctored animals, and told jokes. We had a neighbor, Mr. Everett Van Den Bros, who knew how to do most everything else. He was a plumber, electrician, bricklayer, and all-around nice guy. If Dad couldn't do it, Mr. Van Den Bros could and was always willing to help.

In the summer, when brother Don and I were not in school, we were awakened each morning by the sound of Dad. "Okay, boys, rise and shine, we have work to do," all in a very loud, commanding voice. Usually, the work involved tobacco, doing things such as worming, suckering, or hoeing. Late summer, it was pulling tobacco and all the other things involved in getting the tobacco hung in the barn for curing. We put the tobacco on sticks to be hung across the timbers in the barn—my job. Another was harvesting corn. Another summertime chore was getting up hay for storage in the horse and cattle barn.

Although Dad was a stern taskmaster, he was always telling or pulling a joke on someone, often his boys. He smoked a pipe, and he would try to trick me into thinking he could make smoke come out from around his eyes so I was to watch his eyes closely as he proceeded to burn my hand with his hot pipe. (Just to startle me, not really burn). Well, he was not the only one who could play tricks. I decided that I would get him back for some of his tricks on me by coming up with some of my own. Quite often on Sunday afternoons, he would take a little nap in his chair. They were probably well-deserved naps, but I had to trick him, so I dreamed up a really good plan. I got some of his shaving cream and put a glop of it on the fingers of his right hand, then proceeded to tickle his nose with a feather. At first, he just kind of wrinkled his nose and went back to dreamland. Not to be stopped in my efforts to get him, I tickled his nose again. This time he wiped the big glop all over his face. He didn't realize at first what was happening but when he did realize it he came for me. I believe he was proud that his young son was following in his footsteps.

Once, a cousin came by while we were butchering hogs and mentioned that he loved ribs. Dad said, "Oh, we don't eat the ribs." Cousin Woodrow excitedly said he would like to have them. Dad said "sure, you can have them … as soon as we get the meat off the bones". Dad had a habit of naming newborn calves after friends and would proudly introduce them to their namesake. At one time, Dad had a young man living with us and working for us whose name was Joe, and during that time we had a colt born that needed a name. My brother Bob also was living at home at that time, and I guess Dad didn't know whose name to use: Joe, or Bob. He settled it by using both names, so "JoeBob" became the name.

One of my fond memories of Dad was the Sunday mornings I spent with him in the front yard under a large maple tree reading the Sunday paper. We went to church only one Sunday a month because our traveling preacher only came once per month. We only got the Sunday paper, because the other days of the week were work days and we had no time for the paper. This was when I was very young, and the extent of my reading or looking was the comics. He always got to them first, so I waited anxiously for him to finish. I still read the comics today but now read the other sections too.

One should never underestimate the value of a good partner, and the sharecropper had the best: my mother, Rosie. She was a wonderful wife to my dad and a wonderful, loving mother to all of us children. She was the glue that held the family together. Mom was many things to Dad and to all us boys. She was mostly the disciplinarian, confidante to all of us, medical dispenser, teacher, and so many other things that it would take too much space to write about. She always seemed to think that one remedy for most all our ailments was that greasy, smelly, vile-tasting oil from the castor bean, "castor oil." As I sit here writing, I swear I can both smell and taste it, even though I've not even heard that word for years. I remember one particular time when I was feeling poorly, and out came the bottle of castor oil. Right away, I decided that I was not going to drink that terrible stuff and said so immediately. Well Mom was just as adamant as I and demanded that I get on with it, and with nothing to help kill the taste. I still refused. She told me to go out and get a switch from that bush out in the backyard to be used as her enforcer. Like the obedient son that I was, I went out and got a switch which was dead, and it shattered upon contact with my rear, as was my intention. After we both had a good laugh, I took the medicine, I guess out of respect for "Doctor Mom." That was my last encounter with the dreaded castor bean oil.

Another of her home remedies was a taste of whiskey, another medicine that I didn't like. Well, at the time, at least. Dad would occasionally buy a bottle from the ABC store, or sometimes a jar from a friend, who made his own, and Mom would always pour some into a small extract bottle to save for colds. The family accused her of having too many colds herself.

Mom was a loving mother, and her love was never in short supply for all the family and others. She always spoke lovingly of "her boys," and as we all grew up each of us would try to get her to say she loved that particular one the most. Her answer was, "I love all my boys the same." My claim was that, "I am the baby of the family, and I know you love me the most." Didn't work.

To the sharecropper and his wife, I say, "Well done."

The Sharecropper and his wife

Grandpa Burcham

The Sharecropper and his tobacco

Grandpa Billy Buck Martin's Family
Back row, 3rd from the Right: The Sharecropper

Grub Hill Girls- Rosie Burcham Martin
(The Sharecropper's wife) on the right

Chapter 3:
TOBACCO FARMING

Tobacco, being the main cash crop, was very important, and extreme care was taken to ensure that the crop was a good one that would produce lots of good tobacco to sell in the fall. The tobacco we raised was of the bright tobacco variety, which was used mostly for cigarettes. Other varieties were used for cigars or pipe tobacco. To say that tobacco farming was a year-round job would not be too far from the truth. It started early in the year with preparing a plant bed where seeds would be sown to grow the plants to be planted in the tobacco field and didn't end until late fall of the year, when the tobacco was taken to market and sold.

Tobacco has a long history, probably starting with the indigenous people of what is now the North American continent, possibly as early as 6,000 B.C. The American Indians were smoking it when the Europeans settled here, and they introduced it to the settlers. The colonists not only used tobacco but found that it could be gold, after introducing it to the people of Europe. They started shipping tobacco to Europe around 1614 and eventually shipped millions of pounds each year. I've read that in the 1680s they were shipping as much as 25,000,000 pounds per year. If cotton became king in the southern states, as in "King Cotton," tobacco was king in the states of Virginia and North Carolina. It certainly was the main cash crop in Virginia, where I grew up. Unfortunately, tobacco and cotton crops were a main reason for slavery coming to America because of the labor-intensive nature of tobacco and cotton, which would make producing them too expensive without free labor. Much of the growing and harvesting of cotton and tobacco is now done with machinery, without the hand labor of years ago.

My father was involved in growing tobacco just about all his life, from his birth on his father's farm until he retired and sold his farm, just a few years prior to his death at age 79. He had done everything one can do with tobacco, including smoking it in his ever-present pipe. He quit smoking "cold turkey" at age 75, after deciding that smoking might not be good for his health.

Following are my memories of how bright tobacco was grown on our family farm as I was growing up. The methods have changed a lot with modern machinery doing much of the hand work that we did, but the results are the same.

The Plant Bed

The plant bed was where the plants were grown from the seeds saved from the previous year's crop. This was started in February or March with the soil plowed and smoothed very level; the seeds were distributed evenly. The soil was raked to cover the seeds, and then it was all covered with cheesecloth. The cheesecloth was used to assure that the plants were kept warm in the chilly air. After the plants took root and the air was warm, the cover would be removed in order to expose them to the sun and to acclimate them to the air where they would soon be planted in the field.

The Planting

In the spring, after the soil warmed a bit, the field was prepared with the rows being mounded in preparation for the plants to be set. Most often, we used a wooden peg to make a hole in the ground for the plant. If the ground were really dry, we would use a hand held device called a planter which had a water tank on it. Using this method we would drop a plant into the planter, make a hole in the ground with the planter, give it a twist and the plant dropped into the soil where the roots were covered with soil along with a shot of water. This was somewhat slower but necessary in dry weather.

Hoeing, Worming, Suckering, and Sweating

Once the field was planted, it must be cared for by hoeing, which not only gets rid of grass and weeds but also mounds up the dirt to the base of the plants to be sure the roots are covered. After the plants grow a bit, the worms start to work eating the leaves and must be stopped. The tobacco worm is green, round, and filled with green liquid. As they get older, they get horns, and many have white eggs attached to their backs, to assure more worms later. They must be stopped from eating the cash crop, so we would pull them off and kill them. I remember the first time I had to do that, I asked Dad how to kill them. Being the jokester he was, his answer was, "bite their heads off." Actually I never bit their heads off, but if I had, the nasty green liquid would have run down my chin. I decided to use a different method to kill them, just pull them apart. Of course, that gets the green liquid on your hands. Even better is to throw them down very hard and smash them. If you should ever get the chance to kill them, my advice is to not accept the job. Brother Don and I found how to have a little fun with the worms. We found that if you tie a tobacco string around their fat bodies and tie them to a match box loaded with dirt, they will pull it away. It's fun. Try it sometime.

As the plants grow, suckers come on them, which need to be removed. Removing them allows the leaves to grow larger, which is important since that part is what provides the cash from the cash crop. You can tell by now, tobacco required a lot of handwork and was very time-consuming. Don and I learned to work at whatever was necessary on the farm. I think we are better for the experience. A lot of sweating was done on the farm. Some people pay money to go to a sweat lodge. We got it all for free. We didn't know how fortunate we were back on the farm.

Tobacco Pulling Day

After the tobacco is planted, wormed, suckered, and hoed, it starts to ripen for harvesting. Our bright tobacco started ripening from the bottom of the plant, with the bottom two or three leaves turning yellow, which would be removed at the first of about six or seven "pullings," or sometimes called "pickings." The pulling days always started early in the morning, and as we pulled the leaves, we would put them into a tobacco sled pulled by a horse in-between the rows, and when it was full we took it to the barn where the barn workers would tie the leaves onto a tobacco stick. The sticks would be hung in the tobacco barn. The barn was heated over about a week, and the temperature would be raised gradually over the week to cure or dry it. We had two tobacco barns; one was a log barn and was heated by the burning of wood, and the other was a frame barn and heated by oil burners. As the temperature was raised, it got to about one hundred and eighty degrees, and dad stayed there for the last few nights to be sure all went well. Occasionally, people had tobacco barns burn because of the extreme heat. Tobacco would fall onto the hot flues, igniting the dry tobacco and possibly the barn, which was a costly burn. Both a barn of tobacco and the barn itself, which was needed for the next pulling, would be an expensive loss. If the farmer had only one barn for future pullings and it burned, he was presented with a catastrophe for his later pullings. We were fortunate since we had no barns burn.

After the tobacco was cured in the barn, the heat would be cut off and the door opened so the tobacco would soften some. If it was too brittle, it couldn't be moved, since the tobacco would shatter, and some would be lost. After it was softer, it would be moved to the pack house and stored for some time while other tobacco was pulled and cured until ready to pack away. In late summer or early fall the tobacco in the pack house is unpacked, sorted, and tied together again to take to market for selling. All the methods I'm writing about were used when I was back on the farm. Things change, and this is no exception. Actually, I have no knowledge of today's practices.

The Market Days

The market days were very important to the farmers since it was payday for a year of hard work. Most farmers would go to market only a day or two per year, depending on when their tobacco was ready for market. Most people in regular jobs are paid either weekly or monthly, so just imagine getting paid once or twice each year. In addition, the farmer did not know how much his payday check would be. Tobacco was sold by auction, and the tobacco farmer had no control over the price. They either accepted the offers or didn't sell. The government did have an allotment system which gave each farmer an allotment as to how much the farmer was allowed to grow. This was to control the supply of tobacco on the market, and along with this, the government had price supports and actually bought a lot of tobacco to support the farmer, which is not done today. This program ended in 2005, and thousands of farmers stopped growing tobacco at that time. In addition, many people stopped smoking, so the demand for tobacco has greatly reduced.

The warehouses where the tobacco was sold were huge, with long rows of tobacco stacked up for selling. The auctioneers would go down each row, speaking in a singsong, chant-like voice, along with the farmers keeping watch, and the buyers calling out their bids. Actually, the market days were busy and exciting with the anxious farmers anticipating a big price for their crop. The farmers were anxious to sell for a good price and were looking forward to having some money to take home, often to pay their debts accumulated over the tobacco season. Many started their year out being in debt in preparing for the new crop. Even though tobacco was the biggest cash crop, not many people got rich raising tobacco.

MARTIN FAMILY TREE

This is my family tree, starting with my parents and going back to my great-great-great grandparents.

George Ruffin Martin—born June 29, 1892—died September 9, 1971

Rosa May Burcham Martin—July 29, 1899—died April 31, 1973

They had seven children.

Grandparents

William Wingfield "Billy Buck" Martin—born November 25, 1854—died August 28, 1949

Louise Elizabeth "Betty" Ayers Martin—born June 28, 1861—died November 2, 1951

They had sixteen children. My father was their ninth.

Great-Grandparents

Berryman Jennings Martin—born January 27, 1826—died January 27, 1905

Susan Edwards Martin—born 1832—died 1862

They had four children. My grandfather was their fourth. Berryman's wife died in 1862, and he then married Sarah Ann Andrews, and they had six children.

Great, Great, Grandparents

Samuel H. Martin—born 1797—died 1860

Frances Breedlove Martin—born 1790—died 1860

They had four children. My great grandfather, Berryman Jennings Martin, was their fourth. Samuel's wife died, and he then married Elizabeth Adams Martin, born 1831. They had six children.

Great-Great-Great Grandparents

Richard Martin—born 1758—died 1841

Charity Hunter Martin—born 1760—died 1836

They had eleven children. My great-great grandfather, Samuel H. Martin, was their seventh.

Chapter 4:
EARLIEST MEMORIES
OF GRUB HILL

It's not on any map and there is no sign that indicates the name. There is no evidence, not even the old foundation of Grandpa's store or the house where we lived. Every time I pass by, I look at where it was, and it's like it never existed. When I've passed by with Patsy, my wife, I say, "There's where it was," and I think, well, no, maybe a little farther up that way. We have all traveled country roads and seen a sign with a name that means nothing to us and expecting a country store or some other building. None appears but an old store or another building abandoned. Well, Grub Hill is like that, but with no sign. How can that be when my memories are as vivid as if they happened yesterday? An important part of my childhood was spent there, right over there, I'm sure. In my childhood, that was "Downtown Grub Hill" where my grandpa's store and mill were, and his house was right across the yard. The house where we lived was down a small dirt road behind the store. I used to go up and down that grassy, dusty path, hoping for a handout from Grandpa's cookie bins, some of those ginger snaps or vanilla wafers that were right behind the counter. There is a road named Grub Hill, and down the road a ways is the Grub Hill Episcopal Church, which is still being used. The Grub Hill school on the crossroad is gone. That's where two of my brothers went to the one-room school. I missed out on that school and later went to the school in downtown Amelia. I have my memories but no "Downtown" Grub Hill.

The two-story house where we lived was under several trees and had wooden shingles for siding and a woven wire fence around the yard. Dad tended several hives of honeybees in the backyard. Grandpa sold some honey in his store, and we ate lots of it at our house. I remember when a hive of bees decided to abandon their hive and take up residence in a hollow tree. Dad captured the swarm and placed them in another hive. I was scared then, but many years later, I took up the fascinating hobby of beekeeping.

Down past the old school was my favorite house, Aunt Rosie's. Aunt Rosie was my grandpa's sister and Mom's aunt, and Mom was named after her. Aunt Rosie was the kindest person I ever knew, especially since she loved me so much. More about her later.

Down another road and under a huge oak tree was Trevor Hutchison's blacksmith shop. He had many customers for horseshoeing, since a lot of farmers, like my dad, used horses to farm instead of tractors. Of course, he did other ironwork, too. The shop was a hangout for many of the neighborhood men. Although I was very young, I do have some good memories of living at Grandpa's and of Grub Hill.

Chapter 5:
GRANDPA BURCHAM
AND HIS STORE

Now, back to "Downtown Grub Hill" and Grandpa's store. Burcham's Store. First, Grandpa was my mother's father. She and her brother, my Uncle Charlie, always called him Pa. He had a real grandfather's moustache complete with handlebars and all. His was always brown with the stains of his ever-present snuff, and if he had been drinking buttermilk, there were yellow specks of butter from him straining his buttermilk. Grandpa always wore his sort of uniform of khaki pants held up with wide suspenders and a flannel shirt, which he wore every day, wherever he happened to be. I truly don't recall ever seeing him wear anything else, except on Church Sundays.

Grandpa was born in Springfield, Illinois, where he married Polly Ann Blackburn, a full-blooded Cherokee who died after giving birth to my mother and her brother Charlie. Her Cherokee ancestors had been force-marched to west of the Mississippi River from their home in the Southeastern United States. Approximately 60,000 Native Americans, including Cherokee, Creek, Chickasaw, Choctaw, and Seminole were relocated from their homes in a cruel march, with a death toll of about 4,000 of them on the way. This has come to be known as the "Trail of Tears" because of the deaths of so many by disease, cold, hunger, and just generally bad treatment while on this march. The Cherokee people were educated and peaceful. They appealed to the Supreme Court for relief and won their case; however, President Andrew Jackson refused to enforce it. "The Trail of Tears" started in 1831 and finally ended in 1839. Certainly not a badge of honor for Jackson, or the country as a whole.

Grandpa later married Malinda, whose maiden name I don't know. They moved to Carroll County, Virginia, and later to Amelia County, Virginia, where he started his store. Grandma Malinda never seemed to be a happy person and complained about everything. It was usually the weather, her teeth, her back, the time of year, or just generally feeling bad. I do wish I had been a little older so I could have been more understanding … I guess.

Grandpa's store was a place I loved to visit. It had stacks of just about anything a person could want or need, such as canned goods, a pickle barrel, cracker barrel, big boxes of ginger snaps and vanilla wafers, and cold soft drinks. My attention was usually on the boxes of cookies, and I was not above taking a few when I could get away with doing it. Grandpa always took his lunch at home across the yard, after he locked the front door and went out the back door. Well, I decided that may be a good time to take a few cookies for myself. When he went out the back door and walked away, I was lurking nearby and went in the door and began to help myself to those ginger snaps. As I filled my pockets, I heard the back door open and the floor creak. Uh-oh, I was about to get caught. Grandpa was back, so I ran for the front door, forgetting that the screen door might be locked. It was. As I ran face-first into the locked door and clumsily unlocked it and ran for my life, I heard him say, "Hey, boy. What are you doing?" I didn't wait to say what I was doing. He obviously knew who the little blond-headed thief was but never mentioned my transgressions to anyone, to my knowledge, and surely not to me. What a nice grandpa. All should be so good. I've tried to remember that as my grandchildren have grown up. So much for my early life of crime.

In addition to the store, he had a grain mill where he would grind wheat and corn for the local folks. My mom made her wonderful cornbread, which I dearly loved and still do, from cornmeal ground at that mill. Hot corn bread with fresh butter is really fantastic, and cold corn bread crumbled up in cold milk is even better.

Grandpa also sold gasoline using the old-fashioned pumps, which had to be hand-pumped up to the glass tanks on the top, and then gravity fed the gas into the car tanks. I believe the gas was Texaco's Fire Chief. I'm not sure if he ever changed from those pumps to the more modern types. My guess is that he never did.

He had an old International truck he used to haul an occasional calf or pigs to market for folks around Grub Hill. His driver's side window stayed dirty with the brown stains of snuff from spitting out the window. In the wintertime he would slide the window down just a bit to spit and always missed getting it all out so his spit dripped down the window. He either didn't see it or didn't care. I always enjoyed riding with him to market. Good memories. Well, maybe not so much the spit.

Chapter 6:
AUNT ROSIE

My Aunt Rosie's house was just through the woods from our house and close to the one room elementary school. She lived in a small frame house with a screened porch on the front and a woodshed in back, and, of course, the outdoor toilet or outhouse, as we all had, a little further back at the end of a well-worn path. Aunt Rosie (or Ain't Rosie, as I called her) was the sweetest person you could ever meet. She always thought of the other person's feelings rather than her own. The best thing about her was that she loved me completely and showed it every time I saw her. I had other aunts, but she was my absolute favorite. . When Mom went to see her, I went along, partly because I knew she would always have a treat for me. Her usual was brown sugar and butter on a biscuit. She really loved for me to ask for it because I called it brown "tuger."

In addition to Aunt Rosie, there was her husband, Uncle Alec, her daughter, Cousin Vadie, and son, Sherman, all living together. As I remember, none worked, although I didn't wonder about it until I was much older, when I did begin to think about it. To this day, I am still puzzled about how they existed without working. My dad told me a story about Uncle Alec, which I assume was true, but Dad was fond of making up stories. Dad was plowing with his horses, and Uncle Alec was walking along beside him with his ever-present cane when the plow hit a yellow jacket nest. To say the least, they were not happy about the intrusion, and they, of course, came flying out to check on what had happened. Dad let the horses go so they could avoid getting stung. Uncle Alec threw down his cane and ran "like hell" across the plowed field so he wouldn't get stung. True? Don't know for sure, but it's a good story.

Uncle Alec did do some trapping of various animals to supplement the family food supply. One time he caught a possum, put it in a cage, and fed it corn to fatten it up some, and also to add some flavor to the meat. They didn't invite me to the possum dinner. Thank Goodness.

Their daughter, Cousin Vadie, was a wonderful person, just like her mother, and very smart. She had been crippled as a child by polio, which was referred to as "infantile paralysis," and she could not walk and had limited use of her hands. Although she was crippled in both hands and both feet, her mind was especially sharp, and she was the brains of that family. No real family decisions were made without her input. In addition, she was as pleasant a person as one could find. She was an adult when I came to know her, and we children were told to call her "Cousin Vadie" as a title of respect, and we all did respect and love her. Years later and after her parents died, she had no place to live, and my mom convinced Dad to let her live with them. He was not too happy about that but consented to it. Several months later, when she was admitted to a nursing home, even Dad was sad to see her leave. She was a wonderful person and most pleasant to be around, especially considering her physical condition. She would listen to Dad's stories and his tricks any time and smile and laugh, which delighted him. I guess she was literally a "captive audience".

Chapter 7:
THE HOME PLACE

The home place was where my brother Don and I grew up. He was about nine and I was about seven when we moved to our new home place. The older brothers had already left home. For the sharecropper, this was both the end and the beginning. The end of sharecropping and a new beginning of owning his own farm again. He had lost his first farm because he wasn't able to make the mortgage payment .This was during the Great Depression, and although many farmers had lost farms, this was very personal to him. He had come from a family that owned their farm and depended on no one except themselves.

This new farm had one hundred and sixty acres of land, a very nice house, and several outbuildings, although the outbuildings were eventually torn down because of their bad condition. There was a well with a pump out on the edge of the back yard. Although isolated, it was at the end of the sharecropper's rainbow and was as close to heaven as he had ever been. Many outbuildings were added soon after moving to the home place: a cattle barn with loft, chicken house, grain house, two tobacco barns, another house for brooding chickens, and finally a smokehouse for smoking pork. We dug a new well right off the back porch, near the root cellar. A tobacco pack house was added to store cured tobacco, for later grading and then selling. The former sharecropper was in business.

The house was surrounded by several large trees. First upon the approach to the house was a cedar tree, which was encircled by the driveway.

Then an old rotting cherry tree that soon came down. The ones I especially liked were the large maple trees with big limbs just made for a young boy to climb. I liked to climb all the way to the top and call for Mom to come see me. She always said, "Come down from there, Alton, before you fall." Just what I was expecting she'd say. In the backyard were two walnut trees, which provided lots of walnuts each year.

My personal favorite features of the house were the porches, which ran all the way across the front and the back of the house. The family loved both porches and I have many fond memories of them. The front porch had a wonderful swing, which would easily fit three people, and if we wanted to squeeze in tight, it would fit four. This was particularly nice if some of our friends, who were pretty girls, happened to be with us. Good memories were made in that swing. Most of the time it was Mom and Dad who sat there talking while Don and I were in the yard playing.

The back porch was entirely different, although the family did sit there and talk sometimes. That porch had piles of wood for the kitchen stove and fireplaces, various farm tools and the milk separator. Also the door to the root cellar, which we dug, was there and later, the new well was at the corner of the porch. The cellar was for storing home canned food, potatoes—both sweet and white ones, onions, apples, and anything that needed cool storage.

The house had four large rooms separated by a wide hallway that went from the front door all the way to the back door. Each of the rooms had either a fireplace or a stove. We had screen doors at both ends, which in good weather, created a nice breezeway. After a while a curtain was added in the middle to hide an icebox and other cabinets. When we got electricity, a refrigerator was added to the back hallway, replacing the icebox. That left the front hallway nicer for our company to see.

Chapter 8:
MORNING ON THE FARM

All is quiet, except for the birds that can't seem to wait for the sun to rise and start their day. Patches of light fog hang over the low spots in the pasture and hay fields. There is a slight reddish glow in the eastern sky, which means the sun will soon burn the dew off the trees, bushes, and grass. The farmer, carrying milk pails, leaves a trail as he walks through wet grass heading to the cattle barn, his boots already wet. He reaches for the barn door, and it opens with a creak. He takes the kerosene lantern off the nail where it has hung for years, raises the globe, and lights the wick. He notices the soft, familiar smells of hay and the cows turning toward him and giving him a soft moo in greeting. They know that he will soon relieve their swollen udders, and give them a bucket of wheat bran to eat, which will help them make more milk for the night milking. The man feels the comforting warmth given off by the cows on this chilly morning. The two big work horses stand very still, waiting for some hay and maybe a few ears of corn. They know that they will soon be pulling the plows, opening up the reddish-brown earth for another crop.

The man gets his milking stool and sits down to the first cow, with the metal milk pail placed between his knees to begin milking. The stream of milk hits the bottom of the metal pail with a pinging sound, which soon changes to a fluffy sound as the pail starts to fill with the rich, warm milk. His deft hands make short work of the milking. Then he will be on his way to the milk room on the back porch where the milk separator is located. He will pour the milk into the separator where the milk and cream are separated. The cream will be used to make homemade butter or will be sold to the nearby Farmville Creamery. This will be repeated for the night milking, except "the boys" will be squeezing the udders after they are home from school.

Before the farmer could sit down to a tasty breakfast of bacon, eggs, biscuits, gravy, and coffee prepared by his wife, who had also gotten up early, he would go into his sons' room and with a loud, commanding voice say, "All right, boys, it's time to rise and shine." They got up.

By the time the boys got home from school the man had been in the fields with the horses, plowing all day, and was surely tired from a full day's work.

The man ... my dad. The time ... long ago

Chapter 9:
THE KITCHEN

The kitchen was like the hub of the wheel to the spokes—it kept all the rest together. It was, by far, everyone's favorite. In winter, it was the warmest room in the house because of the Southern Comfort wood burning cook stove. It was most often hot, waiting for Mom to cook something tasty. Quite often that would be chicken frying or cornbread baking, just two of my many favorites. Mom used her cast-iron pots and pans for her cooking, baking, and frying. I remember those pans hot with lard sizzling waiting for something delicious to be cooked. She baked biscuits or cornbread for every meal, unless there were plenty left over. My favorite bread was and still is cornbread, either hot or cold. I liked it hot with Mom's homemade butter or cold with milk and crumbled in a bowl like cereal. I still love it fixed any way it can be fixed. I didn't know at that time, but we have the indigenous people of what is now northwestern Mexico and southwestern United States to thank for our good old cornbread, since they introduced it to our colonists. Thank you. Thank you. The corn for cornbread and the wheat for biscuits were grown on the farm and ground by Grandpa Burcham or by the Beaver Pond Mill. Excuse me. I'm going to make some cornbread now.

The kitchen was large and very definitely an eat-in kitchen with the wood cook stove, large family size table, various cabinets, a pantry under the stairs to the attic, with the flour barrel, cornmeal, and always the one big bottle of whiskey that Dad had for colds and such. Nothing like homemade remedies—doctors were expensive and too far away.

The kitchen ceiling was high, like the other rooms. The floor was made of heart pine and covered mostly with linoleum. Next to the stove was the wood box, which was refilled daily by Don and me. Gathering wood was a small price to pay for the wonderful time in the kitchen had by all. The room had three big windows—two overlooking the back porch, and one over the sink.

In the winter Dad would come in from the field or the barn with cold feet, and he would open the oven and try to get away with putting his feet either in the oven or on the door to the oven. That was not to happen if Mom saw him. She didn't want his feet where she cooked the family bread. He never ceased trying, though.

Also in the kitchen was a steep stairway to the large attic which was seldom used, although some things were stored up there, such as the old letters that Dad had written to Mom when they were courting. Don and I discovered them one time, and, of course, read them all. We found that Dad did have a romantic side to him, and we were both interested and pleased. One we read was not original but it did the job. It read, "Roses are red, violets are blue, I wished you loved me like I love you." I guess she must have, since she stayed married to him until he died.

Another use for the attic was drying apples, which were used to make what we called "flapjacks." I guess today we would call them apple turnovers, but whatever one calls them, they were tasty.

As we all know, times have changed over the years in many ways. Nowadays, the children get to eat first, but when I was a child, if we had company, especially if the company happened to be the preacher, the children had to wait for the adults to finish eating. He seemed to pride himself in how long he could pray as he said grace. Well, you can imagine how much fun it was to see the fried chicken serving plate getting almost empty as our mouths drooled and our stomachs ached and growled. I guess we were like a dog watching each piece of chicken disappear time after time. The preacher seemed to be the biggest eater at the table, and I would see him reach for another piece as I prayed—don't get that breast piece. He did. Well, the kitchen was my favorite room, in spite of the preacher and other adults making me wait.

One of the things I liked was when we had adult company and they talked about stories of their past. Sometimes I'd hear someone ask, "How long has it been since you've seen old Sam?" Or it could be any name. Dad or Mom would look at the ceiling, rub their chin, and I'd hear, "Hmm, gosh, I guess it's been forty years." I'd think, forty years? I'm ten years old. I can't imagine forty years. Well, in recent years, when I was probably sixty years old, at our Martin reunion, I was visiting with my cousin, Franklin. I asked him how long it had been since we had seen each other. He looked up, rubbed his chin, and said, "I guess it's been forty years." That conversation has been about twenty years ago. Seems like such a short time ago.

The kitchen really was used more than any other room and holds more memories. Most of my memories from the kitchen were from around the table covered with food. Family gatherings were some of the best times. Being the youngest of six sons, I was always home, and so was my next older brother, but occasionally all the brothers would be home along with their wives and children. Those were good times. You can imagine the noise with all the family trying to get the attention of all the others. We were taught to say, "thank you for the potatoes," or whatever dish we wanted passed to us. One time when we were all together, I asked for the potatoes without saying, "Thank you for the potatoes," and my oldest brother George told me to say it. I refused and my mom said to say it and I still refused. I never got the potatoes. Oh, well, I'd probably had enough anyway. My dad always said that the best diet was to push away from the table. Guess I was on a diet. Even when I didn't always get my way, our family meals were great in that wonderful old kitchen.

Chapter 10:
OUT BUILDINGS
ON THE FARM

Every farm has a lot of outbuildings out of necessity. Buildings such as horse and cattle barns, grain buildings, and some specific to the type of farm, crops, etc. When my parents bought the last farm they owned, where I grew up, it had been owned by Dr. Eggleston, who had not lived there for several years. All the buildings were really old and would be unusable except the home, which was overgrown with wisteria vines but otherwise very livable. Dad tore down the buildings that were in bad shape and replaced them. About seventy five yards from the house was an old building, which had been used to store grain, although I doubt that Dr. Eggleston used it. It was not usable, so Dad burned it down one night and found it occupied by several families of rats. Being so old, it was dry and burned easily, and created a horrendous blaze. Dad had foreseen possible problems with the fire, so he had some others around to help. Mr. Van Den Bros was with us, brothers Bob, Don, me, and our faithful dog. Spot turned out to be a very valuable member of the team. As the fire burned, the rats abandoned it in large numbers. Spot, of unknown breed, caught and killed so many rats that we could not keep a count during the rampage, however, sixty-three rat bodies were counted at the end, and he killed most of them. He was a rat killing machine, for sure. We all looked at Spot with a new, well deserved respect after that night.

Since we would be having a harvest of corn and wheat later, a new grain building would soon be needed and was built. This one was built on stilts about three feet high, made of terracotta, which was supposed to be unclimbable for rats, and for the most part worked, though not totally, but a big help.

Another building on the farm that was behind the house had been used as an office by the doctor. It was filled with old medicine bottles and all kinds of gadgets pertaining to his medical practice. That building was also in bad condition and was torn down rather than burned because of its closer proximity to the house and the danger of flames reaching the house.

Over time, many additional buildings were built: two tobacco barns, one horse and cattle barn, two chicken houses; one chicken brooder house for raising chickens; one tobacco pack house, where cured tobacco was stored for grading and later sale; a smoke house for smoking meat; and, of course, an outhouse for other necessities, later replaced by an indoor one. Finally, an indoor one. Living, as they say, "high on the hog."

Chapter 11:
LOG BARN RAISING

It's doubtful many people today have seen an old-fashioned barn raising, except maybe in movies. On the farm where I grew up, I did have three occasions to see several friends, neighbors, and family gather together in harmony to build two log barns and one frame building for my dad. I say in harmony because the atmosphere was one of joyful camaraderie, with playful jokes all around. The men seemed so happy to be there, helping. Some of them had been helped with building their own barns, and this was a chance for them to pay back for their help. Even if that was not the case they were still happy to help a fellow man. It was just something people did back then. It was work, but, more importantly, it was fun working together. I remember some of the men trying to say they knew best how to do various parts of the job and others were saying they knew best. All in fun.

The brothers in Amelia were Joe, John, Charlie, Sam, Tom, and, some years later, Rufus. Although I was too small to help, I loved being around them and hearing brothers, and others, having so much fun. Dad had already cut the trees and "snaked" (the term for pulling the logs out of the woods with horses) the logs out near the horse and cattle barn site. The notches for the corners were cut with axes for joining all the logs together and then were raised in place. The barn was two-story, with the top floor serving as storage for hay and the ground floor for the cow and horse stalls. The walls were in place and the roof on at the end of the day, and the men went home to do their own chores. It was fun watching the walls rise steadily throughout the day, and later the roof added. This project was not just a man project, but included my mom and some of the brothers' wives. The ladies prepared some of the best food this side of heaven, including fried chicken, cornbread, biscuits, vegetables and tea. Although I was not old enough to help raise the barn, I did help in eating that wonderful food. It was my pleasure being of service.

Sometime later, we had two more barn raisings. These were tobacco barns. The first was built of logs and was designed to use wood in heating. The second one was frame built and used fuel oil in heating. Barn raisings are a lot of fun and if you have an opportunity to participate I recommend jumping at the chance. Of course, in my case I was only an interested party, not an active participant. That makes it a lot easier.

Chapter 12:
THE OUTHOUSE

Now, I realize that not many people reading this have ever used an outdoor toilet. You may have used a more modern one at some outdoor event, where there was no indoor facility, but not what I would call a real one. Not only did I use one, but I've helped build one. I don't say this with any amount of pride, but just to say, "I've been there and done that." This was in my earlier days back on the farm, when that was the only option. In case you want to build an outhouse someday, for some strange reason, I'll give you a few hints. In building one, there are several things that you need to consider. Location is very important. You want it to be close enough to your house so you don't have to walk too far to get things done; however, you don't want it so close that everybody knows your business. Of course, it should always be behind your house, again, so folks don't see every time you go, especially the women in your family, because they may go several times each day. Guys, of course, don't need an outhouse every time, since any old tree can serve most of our needs. Actually, under a tree can be a good location, unless it's an apple tree or a walnut tree where you may be disturbed by falling fruit onto the tin roof. By the way, the absolutely best roof is the tin roof. It is especially nice when it's raining, except, of course, for the going to it and then going back to the house. Take an umbrella. You may want to consider paint for the outside, although we never painted ours, but if you do decide to paint it, try a color that will blend in and not cause a lot of attention. Oh, by the way, don't build it uphill from your well. Underground streams go downhill. No mixing.

After you've decided on the location, you need to consider the actual style. Some people build a two-seater, but I prefer a one-seater since I consider my business to be just that, my business. Actually, we always had a two-seater, but as far as I can remember, we never shared. I have seen two- and three-seaters, perhaps designed for large families or public use, like churches. The seats should be just like the more modern indoor ones, as comfortable as possible, for your peaceful visit. Another very important thing to consider is whether you'll have real toilet paper or some other paper. In my youth on the farm, it was the pages of the oldest Sears, Roebuck catalog we had on hand. I suggest real toilet paper, if at all possible. A bucket of lime is good for spreading down the hole to reduce any unpleasant odors. The roof should be slanted for rain runoff. The door should have an inside lock so no one is disturbed while busy. Of course, it should be vented for obvious reasons, and for décor a half-moon is typical and nice. Oops, I've overlooked one other important item. The building should be built on sleds for easy moving. You can't use the same hole forever, so it will need to be moved to a new location at some time. No need to pick the building up, just pull it to the new hole. You will need to dig a new hole and be sure to fill in the old one. No one wants to fall into that old one.

Chapter 13:

SEARS, ROEBUCK CATALOG

"Oh, boy, here comes a Sears catalog." We were all, from the youngest to the oldest, excited to see the big "wish book" come in the mailbox. It had just about anything one could want: clothes and shoes, toys, medical and veterinary supplies, musical instruments, bicycles, sewing machines, baby buggies, guns, appliances, radios, Allstate cars, scooters, all kinds of farm supplies. The catalog was about two or three inches thick, and it arrived in our mailbox free. We drooled over it for the whole year, until the next one came, and then used the pages of the old one for "other" things. Then, it began all over again for the next year.

One big reason we were so excited over a catalog was that we hardly ever went to any store to shop. Transportation to Richmond from our very rural Amelia County was difficult, to say the least, and as I think back, it couldn't have been as good as a big old Sears catalog. Dreams galore!

We boys learned early in life to hunt squirrels, rabbits, and birds, using shotguns. I remember well my first shotgun, which was ordered and arrived in the mail from Sears. It was a J.C. Higgins, twelve-gauge, bolt/ action, held six shells without the plug, which came with it and restricted it to three shells. It did the job well.

We even ordered shoes from the catalog, even if they didn't fit exactly. Pants and some shirts came from the catalog. Once, shoes came in the mail for me and were too small for my big feet. I expected them to be sent back, but Mom had other ideas about it. She filled the shoes with kernels of corn, tied the shoes tightly, and added water, with the expectation that the corn would swell, and so would the shoes, and expand to fit my monster feet. Actually, they did expand some, but not to my satisfaction, but wear them I did. I believe that was where I got the name "Bigfoot."

Sears was certainly ahead of the times with their catalog shopping. It sure filled the need for rural America, due to the limited transportation of us country folks. Unfortunately, they later added stores and apparently had no experience in store shopping, and they are now out of business. Amazon seems to be filling that need, but to those of us who remember those big "Wish Books," it's hardly the same. I don't see the excitement in looking online for my wishes and needs, although I'm adjusting to online shopping. Nostalgia is wonderful but, I'm looking online … Amazon.com?

Chapter 14:
ELECTRICITY DOWN
ON THE FARM!!!!

Electricity down on the farm! Boy, oh boy, electric lights! What will happen next? I was a preteen youngster when this wonderful thing happened. If you haven't lived in a home without electricity, you can't possibly know how exciting this event was for us. Prior to this, we lived with old fashioned oil lamps. Brother Don and I did our homework sitting close to an oil lamp, our mother did her sewing by the dim light of oil lamps, and Dad did his reading by them. We had lights at the flip of a switch instead of taking off an old sooty globe, turning up the wick, striking a match, putting the globe back on and then readjusting the wick. I remember well when the overhead lights were installed, and our lives changed forever.

Yes, electric lights in our home, the chicken houses, the cattle and horse barn, the grain house, and another light on a high pole that illuminated all around the outbuildings. We were living in "high cotton." In addition to lights, we had indoor plumbing, which would be impossible without power. No more outhouse trips in the middle of the night. Prior to this, we made extensive use of oil lanterns, which were carried everywhere we went at night. Also, no more iceboxes. We had a real electric refrigerator, used, of course.

This electrification took place in 1948, and this was late, but not as late as you may think. There were some rural areas that didn't get electricity until even later. In 1935, President Franklin Roosevelt signed an executive order establishing the Rural Electrification Administration (REA). It was found that only about ten percent of rural homes, which were mostly farms, had electricity. The REA was intended to "rectify and electrify" that situation. By 1970, about 99% had electricity, so it worked well. The REA loaned money to rural electric cooperatives (ours was the Southside Electric Cooperative) to help electrify rural America. Keep in mind that when the REA was established, America was still in the Great Depression and a great many people were still out of work with little or no money.

Since we lived about a mile off the road, big poles had to be put up to hold the wire from the road to our house, and they cost money, so Dad made a deal with the electric cooperative that he would provide the poles and they would install them. One thing that we had plenty of on the farm was trees, so Dad cut cedar trees to serve that purpose, and Southside Electric installed them and hooked us up to power.

Mr. Van den Bros had already wired the house and put fixtures all over the house and other buildings, so we waited for the power, which seemed to take forever, but finally came. And, presto, power arrived, and the lights were on. Glory days were here! Brother Don and I turned the lights on and off over and over again until our parents turned us off, even though they were just as excited as we were but just didn't respond the same.

The former sharecropper not only owned his farm but had become more modernized, which helped to reduce his burden of being a farmer. I'm sure his pride was enhanced greatly by this accomplishment. He was taking care of his family better than he had before. Times were good.

Chapter 15:

SKUNK IN THE
CHICKEN HOUSE

One night after we were all asleep, I was awakened by a noise coming from outside. I listened intently to determine the source. Strange, but it sounded like chickens squawking. Yes, that's what it was, chickens squawking, for sure. I didn't hear anyone else getting up from bed, so I figured I would have to check it out. Putting on my pants and shoes, I trod out to the chicken house, using our new outside light to guide me. I turned on the chicken house light to see chickens running around in a real panic, sort of like a chicken with its head cut off, which I had seen many times, as Mom prepared for Sunday dinner. It took me a while to determine why they were upset, until I saw a small, black animal running around wild, and as panicked as the chickens. Then I saw a white stripe running down its back, indicating to me that it was certainly a skunk. Yes, definitely a skunk. What to do? What to do? What was I going to do? I know, I'll get my new twelve-gauge shotgun, purchased from the big Sears Roebuck catalog. I thought all that, not out loud, although I don't think the skunk or the chickens would know what I was saying. I ran to the house, got out my shotgun, and loaded it with whatever shot I had close by, then ran carefully back to the chicken house, hoping the skunk was still around so I could be a hero. Yeah, there he was. Taking careful aim so not to hit a chicken, I pulled the trigger, and the skunk was dead and soon the chickens calmed down. Their hero had saved them. They had no idea that this was just delaying their peril, as they would soon be in another situation, in which they would be less likely to escape. Our table would be the next hazard they faced.

Well, this is not exactly the end of the story. Dead skunks smell as bad as live ones, and my trophy smelled really bad in the chicken house. Dad took pity on me and removed the dead skunk the next day. Pew! I decided never to kill another skunk in the chicken house, even if it needed killing.

Chapter 16:
CHURNING BUTTER

Although butter was available from the grocery store, we never bought butter; Mom made it. Not only did she make it for the family, she made it to sell to others. The proceeds were part of her "butter and egg money," of which she was very possessive. She kept it separate from the regular farm income, and she decided exactly how it would be used, sometimes for something special for "her boys." We boys approved.

Butter was churned using heavy cream and some milk in a pottery-type churn about two-and-one-half feet high with a wooden top that had a hole in it for the paddle handle. The handle was raised and lowered by hand for several minutes to churn the cream and milk mixture, and soon the churning would get harder as the butter formed. We boys often helped her with that, if we were not busy in the fields. Her butter was highly regarded as being the best for miles around, along with her eggs, so people would most often come for both butter and eggs. If she didn't use the cream for butter, it was sold to the Farmville Creamery after being picked up on certain days by Mr. Souder at the end of the driveway, which we delivered there in a cream can. The byproduct of churning butter was buttermilk, which some people really liked, including my grandpa Burcham.

After the churning was done, Mom made round cakes of butter, sort of like a small layer cake. She always added a special print on top of the soft butter, which indicated it was Mrs. Martin's butter and therefore especially good. People would come from miles around to purchase her butter. She was a humble person, but she loved the praise for her butter. The same for her eggs, which were often sold at the same time as the butter. The eggs really were farm fresh, and so was the butter.

Chapter 17:
BUTTER AND EGG MONEY

Although tobacco was our main cash crop, we had other ways to add to the family income. We always kept chickens, both for the eggs and for meat, and we sold eggs to people who wanted good, farm-fresh eggs for their tables. The chickens were seldom sold since we wanted the eggs they provided; however, all chickens eventually stop laying eggs. Also, chicken was a staple of our diet, and we wasted nothing on the farm, so if they didn't lay eggs, they became fried chicken for our table. Mom was in charge of the chickens, even the killing and preparation, including the cooking, and she cooked good fried chicken. Since we didn't have a phone, our friends and relatives couldn't call when they wanted to visit, so they would just show up. Mom's brother, my Uncle Charlie, and his family lived near Williamsburg, and they would visit occasionally. They would always come around eleven a.m., just before lunch or, as we called it, dinner. After some brief visiting, Mom would just disappear without a word and go to the chicken house, grab a chicken, and the chicken would lose its head. Not too long after that, we would smell frying chicken. No visits to the grocery store.

The money was added to the family income, especially until the mortgage was paid off. After their family finances were better, she did get a little more independent with her butter and egg money. The "wanted" things would often be something for brother Don and me that we could not usually afford. She loved "her boys."

One time, I remember Mom decided that she wanted a comfortable recliner chair and talked to Dad about it, and his answer was no, they couldn't afford it and she didn't need it. After she discussed that for a while with Dad and got no agreement with him, she announced to him that she was buying one with her butter and egg money, and he was not to sit in it ever. She had had enough talk, and she was taking action. She bought it, had it delivered, sat back, reclined, and smiled. She was happy and again forbade him to sit in it.

Sometime after the purchase of the chair, she had an opportunity to visit some relatives in Ohio, where she had lived as a child. She made her plans to travel there with her brother, my Uncle Charlie. On the day of departure, she had a private talk with Don and me. She told us that she was putting some powder on the vinyl seat of her chair and we should not sit in it, so if the powder was disturbed, she would know that Dad had tried it out, which of course was a no-no.

Sure enough, when she came back, she looked real closely at the seat of her chair and, heaven forbid, the powder was disturbed. When Dad came in from the barn, he didn't even get a chance to say hello before he was "jumped on with both feet," so to speak. Dad wore two hearing aids and had a habit of turning them off when he didn't want to hear something. He turned them off this time, but got the message anyway. Mom was a gentle soul and she eventually forgave him and allowed him to try her new butter and egg chair. Peace was restored.

Chapter 18:
BLACKBERRIES AND CHIGGERS

If you have never been in a blackberry patch picking berries on a hot summer day, you've missed some really good things. You've also missed out on some bad things, mainly chiggers and briars, which go along with berries like "hot and sweat." Those ripe, juicy berries that stain your hands and dribble down your chin are really hard to beat. Now, getting Mom to make some blackberry cobbler and add some homemade ice cream is as close to heaven as is on this earth. We had lots of blackberry patches in the pastures at the sides of the woods. I helped Mom to pick berries many times, but a lot of my pickings didn't get into the pail, nor of course into the cobblers, but in my salivating mouth.

In addition to chiggers and briars, wasps like blackberries just like we do. They hang around the patch too. So, there was competition for those juicy berries, but we always had enough to make pies and can for later in the winter. My mother always tied rags soaked in lamp oil around her ankles because the chiggers start there and climb up your body and often stop in some embarrassing spots, not to be scratched in public. In spite of all the mentioned problems, we always got plenty of berries and had lots of cobblers. Well worth our time and problems. One additional thought about blackberry patches on the farm is that we didn't plant them, fertilize, or care for them in any way. We just picked what God provided for us from His bounty.

Chapter 19:
STUMPS AND DYNAMITE!!!

When Dad bought the old Eggleston place, most of the land was wooded and needed to be cleared so he could grow crops. In addition to selling pulpwood, which was cut by the buyers, we cleared a lot of land by hand. In the early days, we boys were not too helpful in doing this, but as we grew, we were able to do a lot of the work. We used an old-fashioned crosscut saw. The blade on the crosscut was about five feet long and had handles at each end. These handles were pulled back and forth by two men, or, in our case, by two boys. That may sound easy, unless you are one of the men or boys doing the pulling. Actually it was not too hard, unless you continue to pull hour after hour, which we often did. After cutting the tree down, the limbs were cut off and the tree was cut into smaller pieces, usually stove or fireplace length. As we cut the trees to clear the land, we were also providing wood for cooking and heating, thus accomplishing two needs.

Later, Dad bought a power saw, which was on two wheels. Again, it sounds easy. However, the saw was powered but not the wheels, so moving it from tree to tree was not an easy task, especially over rough terrain with cut brush in the way. The round blade was at the end of a gooseneck, which of course would be horizontal for cutting down trees and vertical for cutting the tree into smaller pieces. We finally decided to cut each log into eight-foot pieces and haul them to the wood pile behind the house. Dad built a rack with the saw blade at the end placed vertically. We would move the log along the rack and push it into the blade which would cut the log off at whatever length we wanted. A lot better than cutting the pieces in the field. After we had all the short pieces cut, it was splitting time, which we did with a splitting maul and a metal wedge. Sounds like fun, huh?

Now, back in the cut-over field, we addressed the stumps. The field needed to be cleared of stumps so it could be plowed. We used dynamite to blow them up. Our neighbor Mr. Van Den Bros knew all about dynamite, and he convinced Dad to use it to blow up the stumps. He taught Dad and me how to use it safely, and I was happy and proud that Dad chose me to do the dynamiting. I really enjoyed the experience. The dynamiting procedure: using an auger, bore a hole under the stump ending under the largest part of the stump. Determine how much dynamite you need, one stick or maybe just half a stick, depending on the size of the stump. In addition to the stick of dynamite, you need a blasting cap and a length of fuse. The fuse will be inserted into the hole in the blasting cap, and the cap should be slightly crimped using a wooden stick, so that it will not be dislodged. Do not use any metal such as pliers to crimp it since that could make it explode in your face. The length of the fuse could be determined by how fast you can run after the fuse is lit, since you don't want to be too close when it explodes. Watching it explode from afar is fun. The stump usually goes straight up but could go off to the side, too. One time while Dad and I were working together, he suggested that we try it on a whole standing tree. We put two sticks under it, lit the fuse and ran. We watched the tree lift straight up and then sit back down and remain standing straight. It actually took two years for it to die and fall down.

Dad later decided to hire a man with a bulldozer to finish clearing the field. It cost a whopping $13 an hour. I believe this was in the early 1950s, and things were cheaper then. It went faster but wasn't nearly as much fun.

Chapter 20:
GETTING UP THE HAY

"Make hay while the sun shines." Harvesting hay is a summertime job, so that old saying is not just a slogan; it's real and very important. Weather is always on a farmer's mind, so in addition to many other things, a farmer has to be something of a weather forecaster. He needs to know as well as he can when to plant and when to harvest. Some farmers have an irrigation system, which can provide water for growing crops at the time it's needed. Farmers who don't have such a system have to depend on rain to water their crops. When the farmer wants to harvest hay he needs to know, as best as he can, when sunny days are just ahead with no rain. This is important because after he cuts the grass, he needs a few days of sun in order to dry the hay. It must be dry before it's baled or put into the hay barn. If it's wet or still green, it may mold or could foster combustion and catch fire while stored tightly together, as in a bale or storage area. In addition, if a horse or cow eats moldy hay, it could make them sick, so it's important that it be dry when stored.

On our farm, we fed workhorses and cows hay in the wintertime, when there was not much grass in the pasture. After the hay is cut, as mentioned, it needs to dry before it can be stored, and of course it needs to be stored in a dry place. We stored it in the loft of the cattle barn, which, in addition to being dry, was convenient for dropping hay down to the animals through holes in the loft floor. While storing hay, the loft is a hot dry place and the air is filled with chaff from the dry hay and can be a very unpleasant place.

As the loft starts to fill, it gets really stuffy and space is limited. I often had the job of dragging the hay to the back of the loft, which to say the least wasn't particularly pleasant. Wasps always had nests on the ceiling, and they didn't like me invading their space. They showed their displeasure by circling, ready to swoop on me if I got too close. I never got stung up there, but I always expected they would get me, which may have been worse than actually being stung.

In years when we had a bumper crop and had more hay than the loft would hold, we would build haystacks outside. We had cedar posts about fifteen feet high, and we piled hay around the posts, interlocking the hay around in a circular fashion to tie it together. The top would slope down to the outside so the rain would run off and not soak into the pile, very similar to a thatched roof. We fed that hay before the loft hay since the stack was exposed to the weather and could rot if it stayed there a long time.

Chapter 21:
WHEAT THRESHING DAY

Modern day wheat threshing is done by a machine called a combine, which is driven over the wheat field, cutting the wheat stalks, and then through an internal process separating the grain from the wheat stalk. The grain goes into a bin on the combine or is blown out into an accompanying truck, while the stalk is blown out on the ground. A very efficient way to get the job done. Many years ago, a scythe was used to cut wheat and then the wheat was beaten to remove the grain, and the grain was thrown up into the wind to remove the chaff. This was way before my time, by the way.

When I was a youngster, too young to be of help in harvesting wheat or anything else, it was harvested with a stationary wheat threshing machine. The wheat was cut in the field with a machine, same as the one used to cut hay, pulled by either horses or a tractor, and then picked up by using a pitchfork onto a wagon and carried to the stationary threshing machine. The machine separates the grain from the stalk, just like the more modern combine, and each comes out of the machine, and the wheat is taken to the grain storage bin and the stalks to the hay loft or some other storage area. This machine is basically the same as the combine, with the exception of where the threshing is done. As one can see, this requires a lot of handwork, near impossible to do by a lone farmer. This is when Wheat Threshing Day comes in.

Wheat Threshing Day is a day when several farmers get together and work to help each other in harvesting wheat. Money is not exchanged, just labor. As one may imagine, it is also a day when friends do a lot of visiting and tall stories abound. I don't remember if the owner of the machine was paid in cash or labor exchange. Perhaps he had more wheat to harvest and therefore received more free labor.

Another thing to think about is that farmer on whose land they happened to be at dinner time provided the food for all the helpers. This was great food and fellowship, usually consisting of lots of fried chicken, biscuits, cornbread, vegetables, and ice tea. Everybody forgot about the labor, just thought about the good food. A good time was had by all. I always participated in the dinner part.

Chapter 22:
CUTTING, SHOCKING AND SHUCKING CORN

We harvested our corn by hand, which required a lot of hard work. Today, most all the work in planting, cultivating, and harvesting corn is done by machine, which allows more work to get done in a shorter time and with much less physical work. The planting started in early springtime and the work continued on through late fall or even into wintertime with the harvesting. The harvesting started after the corn stalks were all brown and dry. Even though it was hot, we usually wore long sleeve shirts to guard against the sharp cutting leaves. The cutting was done by using a corn knife, which is similar to a machete with a curved bottom. We would grab a stalk and hold it while we placed the knife at the bottom of the stalk and pull it up towards us to cut. The leaves would shatter and begin to get all over our shirts, and eventually down our shirts. After we cut a few stalks, we would gather some and begin to form shocks, which would be tied around near the top of the shock. The bottom would be spread out so to stand and not fall over. If you haven't seen these in fields, I'm sure you've seen them in pictures in fall scenes. Very pretty, but they don't show the work done to make them so.

One of my "townie" school friends thought cutting corn would be exciting and fun (little did he know) and asked if he could help. We said okay and set a day and time for him to come out to the farm. On the assigned day, he arrived with new boots, work clothes, a brand-new corn knife with the green paint still intact on the blade, and a big, confident smile. All except the smile was from his father's store in downtown Amelia. He was so happy and ready to get started, so I gave him a quick lesson on cutting corn. After a little while, the corn chaff started itching, and sweat started pouring, but he was still enthusiastic and working twice as hard as need be, as anyone would in trying something new. Trying to help him, I was also working twice as hard as I needed to. Dad noticed what was going on and came around and, as nicely as he could, asked him to leave. He took it well and, with his new work clothes dirty and sweaty and the paint on his corn knife scraped a bit, probably his badge of honor, left with some dignity. I am, however, leaving his name out for the protection of the innocent.

After the corn was all cut, the rows of shocks looked nice in the fields. Add a few pumpkins and a black cat or two, and Halloween never looked so good. However, in the late fall or early winter, after the corn ears had fully dried, shucking time would arrive.

This, too, was a job for "the boys," Don and me. A wagon was put in the field for the corn stalks, which were saved for the cows, horses, and pigs to eat. We put the ears of corn in a sled with sides, which was stored in the grain building for later feeding to the horses and cows. The weather was usually fairly cold, so we were dressed with hats, sweaters, coats, and gloves. We tried to keep the gloves on our hands because it was so cold, but it's harder to do the shucking with them on, so we mostly did the shucking barehanded. We would tear the shocks down and do the shucking. We would often be surprised by several mice who had taken a winter home in the cozy shocks. Whole families would go scurrying in all directions as we tore down the shocks, depriving them of a winter home and an endless supply of delicious food. I always felt sorry for them but could not help them.

In addition to feeding the corn to horses, cows and pigs, the stalks were saved to feed the farm animals if the hay ran out. Few things are wasted on the farm.

Chapter 23:
BROOM STRAW DAYS

On a farm, leisure time is scarce; however, when it does come around, it's good to have something to do rather than just sit around. The seasons of the year can provide various activities that are so much fun and make many pleasant memories. One such activity for the fall time was, for brother Don and me, very pleasant. That's Broom Straw Days. Picture a crisp, cool, and sunny fall day and a field of grass with broom straw standing about two feet tall, and slight cool breeze blowing over the broom straw. Now, lie down on your back. The straw will keep the breeze off you, and the warm sun will heat you. Now, look up at a clear blue sky and you'll likely see some clouds being blown around by winds high in the sky, which, if you are creative, will present you with all kinds of shapes for your imagination. Just relax and let your imagination go to work and you will see lions, tigers, dogs, castles, mountains. Add some superheroes if you are into such things. You will be limited only by your imagination. Super cool. Try it. You will love it. If you happen to go to sleep, so what? It will be peaceful. Wait, is that Dad calling? "Boys, come on, we've got work to do." Oh no, he sounds pretty upset. How long can we wait to answer? Time to get up now. Well, it was great while the sun was shining and the breeze was blowing.

On another straw day (not Broom Straw), things didn't work out so well, especially for brother Don. As we mentioned, we always harvested hay not by bales but loosely, except one time we had wheat straw bales stacked out just up from the cattle and hay barn because there was no room in the hay loft. It was important not to have it too near the barn, in case of fire. If one caught fire, it may cause both to burn. Well, on this particular day, a fire did start on the wheat straw bales, so it was a good thing the bales were not too close to the barn. Dad and I were out behind the house when we saw a big black cloud of smoke down by the barn. We rushed down and saw the stack of straw bales on fire. Don was already there, so we all went to work putting the fire out and managed to do so in short order. Many of the bales were blackened by the fire but we saved most of them. As we were finishing up, Dad asked Don if he knew how it started and Don reluctantly said that he had started the fire. Dad asked how it happened.

Meanwhile, I was standing aside while thinking I was so happy it wasn't me trying to explain and thinking that Don was in some kind of trouble. Don explained that he saw several straws sticking out from the bales in a messy sort of way and he decided to straighten them out ... with a match. Oh, boy, Don, you are in trouble, I thought. To my surprise and, I'm sure to Don's surprise and relief, Dad issued no punishment. That incident was never spoken of again. All we could think was that Dad must have done something just as stupid some time in his own past, as we all have, and he may have been forgiven. We all need some mercy, grace and forgiveness at times or maybe all the time. Our Lord knows that and "invented" it just for us.

Chapter 24:
I SAW YOU BREAK
THAT THING
(LESSON LEARNED)

Brother Don and I were constant companions. He was just two and a half years older than me. Most of our time was spent outside early on, playing or later hunting squirrels, rabbits or birds. As we got older, we were busy in the various fields: tobacco, corn, and the big garden. We were usually doing something together, and we always got along great; well, maybe not always. I remember one particular time we had a little problem. I guess one would call it blackmail, as in, do as I say or you are in trouble, boy. Even back then, I loved tools, and Dad had an abundance of tools. He had left one on the back porch, which had a pretty yellow handle. It just fascinated me so much that I picked it up to examine it. At the time, I didn't know what it was, so I just kind of banged it on the porch post and it broke. The tool, not the post. It was a handheld whetstone, used to sharpen knives and such, and I broke the stone. It was a clean break, so I just put it back together and put it back exactly where it had been. That was when I heard a voice (Don's), and he said, "I'm gonna tell Dad you broke that thing." Neither of us knew what to call it. Try as I might, he would not change his mind, so I did his chores for a few days. Don't remember how many. As I did his chores, I would continue to try to get him to relent. No, he would not.

After a while, I decided I would confess my crime to Dad and take my punishment. I went to him with trembling legs with head bowed and said,

"Dad, I broke that thing over there," pointing to the beautiful yellow handled tool. He asked, "What thing?" I showed him and he asked me how I had done it. I told him I had been just playing with it. He looked at it and said, "Well, be more careful next time." And he walked away. I thought, wow, I had expected to be punished. Don had been listening, so he got the news at the same time. I was freed. He now had to do his own chores. I didn't think of grace at the time but have many times after that encounter. I've learned of God's grace and mercy, and I realize that we earthly fathers need to exercise the same grace toward our children and our fellow man as God does for us. What a wonderful lesson I learned that day.

Chapter 25:
MILKING TIME

You may think that milk comes in a carton or glass bottle at the grocery store, and you'd be correct. Not so back in my day on the farm. It actually came from cows, at least it did if you lived on a farm and you had cows that gave milk. Later, when I moved to the city, I was shocked to find that it came in a glass bottle and it was on my doorstep. I don't think it comes on anyone's doorstep now, but the grocery store has lots of it, and in various sizes, shapes and flavors. Sweet milk, butter milk, low fat milk, chocolate milk, skimmed milk, and milk from almonds, soybeans, and who knows what else. Wow, and it used to come only from cows.

We always kept four or five milk cows, and they were milked twice a day, morning and night. Dad always did the milking in the mornings, which allowed Don and me extra time in the mornings to get ready for school. We did the night milking. The cows were always ready for the night milking and were waiting just outside the barn, anxious to get to their stanchion. Each cow had her own assigned stanchion and headed anxiously right to it. (A place their heads went into and were locked in for milking). They were pleased to go in because we had placed feed for them in the manger. We then cleaned their udders, and started pulling on their teats, getting that warm, frothy milk. Summer milking had some especially challenging problems, such as flies and cow tails switching and often hitting the unintended target, our faces. We also received an occasional kick from an unhappy cow, and sometimes knocking over the bucket of milk. Not good.

After the milking was complete, we hauled the milk up to the back porch where we separated the milk from the cream. The separator had a big, pot-like container on top where the milk was poured. It had a spout, through which the milk flowed into and over several disks, which, in some "magical" way, separated the cream from the milk. Actually, it uses centrifugal force and the disks and the different weight of the skim milk and the cream. Below them were two more spouts; from one ran skim milk and from the other ran rich cream. In order for all this to happen, we had to turn a crank-like handle on the machine. Don and I did this job most every night. We either sold the cream to the nearby Farmville Creamery, which they used to make ice cream or other products, or Mom used the milk to make her famous homemade butter. All good stuff.

Chapter 26:
HOG KILLING TIME

Down on the farm we raised or grew just about everything we ate: wheat for flour, corn for cornbread (one of my favorites), even popcorn, all kinds of vegetables, milk and hogs. We didn't have everything we wanted, but had everything we needed and never went hungry, except maybe while waiting for the next delicious meal.

We always had two or three hogs in the pen, and they ate very well all during the year, just waiting for late fall or early winter, which was "Hog Killing Time." You need a good cold day to keep the meat from spoiling while we processed it. Cold weather also meant no flies buzzing around. A few weeks before the day, the hogs were fattened up in order to get maximum meat. On "hog killing" morning, Dad would start a fire under the vat with the "bath" water, which would be used to loosen the hair so it could be removed easier. The vat was about seven feet long and three feet wide, and maybe two feet high. Now, keep in mind that we all eat animals, unless you're a vegetarian, and to my knowledge, the animals are always dead before we eat them. The hogs were killed with a .22 bullet to the head, after which they were left to bleed out for a few minutes. When the hog was ready, we placed it in the hot water for the bath. The water should not be too hot or the hair will set and be hard to pull out. Then if it's too cool the hair will also be hard to pull out. After a little while we began to scrape the hair out. After that, the hog was prepared for cutting up into hams, shoulders, ribs, and pork chops or tenderloin strips. The fat, mostly on the belly, was cut into small pieces for cooking down to make lard, which was stored in five-gallon lard tins for later use in cooking other food. The hams and some shoulders were salted heavily and put up for later smoking, but some of the meat went into the frying pan for that day, along with gravy and biscuits. Some of the shoulders would be ground to make sausage. I've heard people say that they would eat everything but the squeal. Some few people eat the chitterlings, often called chitlins, but we gave them to the buzzards. The chitlins are actually the intestines of the hog, which can be boiled or, more often, deep-fried. This, of course, is after extensive cleaning; however, no amount of cleaning would make me eat them. My thoughts on chitlins are as follows: "Chitlins; boil them, fry them, roast them, never tried them, ain't gonna try them, away we threw them."

As mentioned, the hams and some of the shoulders were salted heavily and stored in the smokehouse. This is not only for preserving but to give them that wonderful salty "country ham" taste. The salt was rubbed into the fresh meat including all the little nooks and crannies to be assured of coverage. The history of salt is old and very interesting. It is even spoken of in the Bible, in both the Old and New Testaments. Jesus said to his disciples, "Ye are the salt of the earth." Salt was and is still very valuable and certainly the disciples were valuable to Jesus in spreading the Gospel of Salvation. In early times, with no refrigeration available, it was especially valuable in preserving meat, fish, and other food items. We humans actually need salt in maintaining our health. The Roman soldiers were sometimes paid in salt rather than currency, so much so that the word "salary" derives from the word salt.

After the hams and shoulders were salted for a few weeks, the meat was thoroughly washed and hung up in the smokehouse. A slow burning fire was built, which provided more smoke than a flaming fire. That job always fell to my mother, and she knew how to do it well, always using hickory wood for good flavor. It's hard to beat good country ham sliced and fried, along with eggs and grits. She would often smoke meat for other people if their meat was ready when she smoked ours. One year, she had several friends' meat to smoke, and that was the only time she ever had a smokehouse fire. The house burned, and most of the meat was lost. She offered to reimburse all, but none took the offer. I remember "hog killing day" as one of the special days on the farm. Yum-yum.

Chapter 27:

HAND-ME-DOWNS
AND OTHER STUFF

If you happen to be the youngest child in your family, you may know exactly what I'm talking about when I discuss "hand-me-down clothes." Being the baby of the family, I was always introduced as "this is my baby boy." I came along the last of six boys, just two and a half years younger than my next brother. One thing this means is that, as the older ones outgrew their clothes, some were still in good shape, too good to throw away, and the Martin family did not throw anything away until it was really, totally, absolutely, positively, used up. The "baby" inherited all of them, with one major exception: shoes. I was and still claim to be the "Bigfoot" of the family. I think my dad had a smaller foot than I did when I was aged twelve. Back to the hand-me-downs. I inherited some faded, worn underwear, pants with holes in the knees and seats and pockets, and shirts but no shoes. They, as well as most other items we bought, came from the Sears, Roebuck catalog, which we called the "wish book," because we all looked and wished a lot, but not too often received.

Actually, living on a farm was a good life, even with older brothers to pick on me. Summers were good on the farm, even when we had to work hard all day in the fields. We spent lots of time outside and the nights outside were special, with the beautiful sky with stars coming out right after supper. There was one thing that was sort of a rite of growing up in the country. That was snipe hunting. Every young boy had to be initiated into this special hunting experience, and the responsibility fell to the older brothers to do this job. We'd all go into the woods, and snipe hunting would be explained. The youngest or the most unsuspecting one (in case we had a townie visiting) would be given a feed sack and told to stay in a certain location, and the others would drive the "snipes" to the sack holder and into the sack. Sounds important to be a sack holder; however, the drivers would then go out of the woods and leave the holder alone. The innocent one would hear every rustling animal, every leaf blowing, or strange noise. By this time, the tricksters were back home laughing and giggling. We never had anyone stay out too long until they finally got suspicious and came back home. By this time, they were initiated and could then look for others to initiate. Fun, huh?

Another hand-me-down was my first bicycle, which was too tall for my short legs, but I was determined to make it work somehow. I lowered the seat, which was way too high. Aha, I jumped on, expecting this to do the job—still too high. Nothing worked, my legs were just too short. I studied and studied and finally I lowered the handlebars and sat on the rear fender and could just barely reach the handlebars. I rode off, sitting on the rear fender and reaching as far as my arms would reach for the handlebars. I've heard it said that necessity is the mother of invention, and I had proved the point as I rode up the long driveway and back repeatedly. The lesson to me was, there is always a way to get something done, if you continue to try, or "you haven't failed till you stop trying". My world had changed. On to the next project.

Speaking of clothes, the farm supply store, Southern States, used to sell chicken feed in special cloth bags decorated with flowers and other designs that were suitable for making shirts and dresses, so, yes, we occasionally would get a shirt made of feed bag material. The good thing about it was that my Mom was an expert seamstress, so it was made well. The bad thing about it was that going to school in a small town, everybody knew about feed bag material at the local Southern States, so it could be a little embarrassing. This reminds me of Dolly Parton and her song, "The Coat of Many Colors." She was very proud, so why should I not be proud, too?

Chapter 28:
HUNTING SQUIRRELS—
HUNTING HOME

Brother Don and I were squirrel hunters early in our lives on the farm where we grew up, probably when I was about ten. Back then, we only had one gun, and that was Dad's old .22 rifle, which may have been around most of his life. Don and I took turns shooting squirrels, well, at least, shooting at squirrels. I'm sure more got away than we took home for Dad to skin. Our prey always heard us coming, walking through the leaves. After they got to know the boys, they didn't seem too scared. They scampered up the tallest trees to get away from us and seemed to have fun at our expense as they jumped happily from limb to limb and from tree to tree, possibly laughing as they gleefully climbed to the sky. Well, regardless of how many we killed, we had fun roaming through the woods and growing up together. Later, we did get shotguns and had a better chance of an actual kill. I don't recall how Don got his first shotgun, but I well remember when my J.C. Higgins bolt action 12-gage that came in the mail from Sears, Roebuck, where we got so many things. I remember the joy I had as I unwrapped it, tearing paper as I hurried to open it.

When I was about twelve years old, the Aaron family moved to a house on the-hard surfaced road near our road entrance. There were four boys and their mother, and Don and I became friends with the two youngest, Calvin and Bobby. They liked to hunt, so we joined up and hunted squirrels together. Their nearby neighbor was the Bernard McMillian family, who had a German shepherd dog that loved to hunt and tree squirrels. Bernard gave the Aaron boys permission to take Jimmy, the dog, anytime they wished. I remember looking up our dirt road seeing Jimmy out front, eagerly waiting to get to work, Calvin coming next, and Bobby bringing up the rear. As they got to our house, we were ready to go. The boys were always polite and would greet Dad and Mom with, "Hello, Mr. Martin" or "Hello, Mrs. Martin."

Off we would go, down behind the barn to the creek, through the tall poplar trees, and take a right turn around the hill going through the big oak trees. Then further through more poplars, where the ruts of the old logging trail were, and then on to the big heart pines. Just a bit further where the pulp wood had been harvested, which had helped pay the mortgage on the farm. We always made the round and managed to get our quota of squirrels and occasionally a rabbit or two. Then back home to brag about our trip, and then skinning time. We all had good times and made many memories.

Well, one trip didn't go as well as usual for me. I was carrying a different gun, for reasons I don't remember, and it got jammed. We all tried to fix it but could not, so after a while I decided to go home rather than just walking along with them. I said I knew how to take a shortcut back home, so I took off. As many times as I had traveled this way, I got turned around and got lost. I came upon two abandoned, dilapidated buildings which I knew were not on our land. That's when I knew I was lost. Also it was beginning to get dark. Adjusting my direction, I continued on and came upon some more unfamiliar landmarks. I was lost, for sure. I finally came up in someone's backyard. The neighbor said, "Howdy." I said, "Howdy" and told him who I was, and he offered me a ride home, which I gladly took. Hunting is fun. Hunting for home, less so.

Chapter 29:
THE LOG CABIN

D on and I decided that we should build our very own log cabin in the woods, not far from the family home. We got permission from Dad and picked out a location which Dad also approved. We talked about it and decided to enlist our two hunting partners, Calvin and Bobby Aaron, who lived a mile or two from us, and they jumped at the idea. All approved, we made our plans for the cabin, got the crosscut saw from its storage place and started cutting down trees. Well, the first tree we cut became lodged in another tree and then the second tree lodged into another and, believe it or not, the third tree also became lodged. That makes three trees lodged, and all were connected. Break time came as we studied the problem while we rested. All of a sudden, someone yelled, "Alton, look out, the tree is falling!" I looked up, and, sure enough, that tree was falling directly towards me. I skedaddled out from under it, as it fell right where I had been resting. No sooner did I get settled again, I heard another yell, "Alton, look out, the tree is falling!" I looked up and another tree was falling toward me. I guess neither tree was happy about being cut down, but why me? I was just one of the cutters. We managed to get the other lodged tree down without any more mishaps. Now, let me say that this cabin was not a second-class cabin, but had two floors. Really first class lodging.

The Aaron boys' older brothers had a small country store nearby, and Calvin and Bobby would bring candy and cigarettes for us from the store. Their Dad was rumored to be a distiller of some fine spirits but did not share with the boys, at least not the two younger ones, so we never had any evidence of that. Might have been good to go with our cigarettes.

Occasionally, Dad would come over to inspect our work, and we could see him coming our way, so we always put our cigarettes out before he arrived. One time after he inspected our work, he walked off about twenty yards, turned around, and said, "Be careful with the cigarettes, don't burn down the woods," left, and never said another word about smoking.

After we finished the cabin, we asked anyone and everyone to come look at it, and all said what a great cabin we built. Oddly, we seldom visited it ourselves. Guess the fun was in the building.

Chapter 30:

UNCLE RUFUS

Uncle Rufus came into our lives when I was about twelve years old. He was my Dad's brother, eight years older and the fourth child of my grandparents, "Billy Buck" and Betty. I first got to know him when he and his second wife, Aunt Jessie, bought some land adjoining our farm. He had lived in Carroll County before he came to Amelia and bought land next to us. He had four children by his first wife and was estranged from them, so he had no help, except for us. The land was all wooded, and we helped him clear the land and helped to build his house and tobacco barn. Whenever he needed help, he would come to our house and ask Dad if the boys could "hope" him for a while. That was his word for help. Dad was very obliging, so off we went. Like most all the Martin brothers, he raised tobacco, which we helped him do.

Uncle Rufus was a short, stocky man with a big belly which shook when he laughed, which was often. Just like my dad, he liked to pull tricks on us children and get belly-shaking laughs at our expense. His face reddened and wrinkled and occasionally he dripped tobacco juice from the ever-present wad of tobacco he chewed. Once when I was helping him cut wood, he stopped and relieved himself and mentioned he knew how to cure an eye infection. I, of course, asked him how, and he said to get up early, relieve myself and rub my eyes vigorously with urine. I expressed my disgust, and he insisted that it worked. I guess that's been about seventy years ago, and I still don't know if it works because I've never tried it. Guess I won't.

After a few years, Uncle Rufus and Aunt Jessie packed up and moved back to Carroll County. We never saw him again. He was nice enough but different.

Chapter 31:
SATURDAY NIGHT AT THE
MOVIES WITH LUCILLE

Yeah, we had a movie theater in little Amelia. In fact, for us teenagers, it was the place to be on Saturday night, after a week of either school or a week of hard work on the farm, if it was summer and we were out of school. I'm thinking of the late forties and early to middle fifties, while we were in our teens. As I remember, the admission was fifty cents, and with popcorn and a coke the total was one dollar or less. We got to see one or two movies with Roy Rogers, Gene Autry, Hop- along Cassidy, Lash Larue, and Zorro, along with news reels of current events. Tom Golden owned the theater and ran it along with his wife and daughter. Some years later, he closed it and started a drive-in theater, which bothered me since I had had a lot of good times there over the years, but it's hard to stop progress, I guess.

Mr. Golden did provide another attraction at his indoor theater that I liked, and that was his daughter, Lucille. She was blonde and cute. I would always sit on the front row, and after a while she would come join me. That was better than the movies. I liked to hold her hand, but I was painfully shy, and it took forever for me to build up the courage to grab her hand. She usually got tired of waiting for me, so she just grabbed my hand. Like West Virginia, almost heaven. She was well worth the wait, but I was seldom able to take the initiative.

Like so many people, after school and a hitch in the U. S. Navy, we lost touch and never saw each other until years later, when I was in life insurance sales. Shy no more, I called on someone in her office where she was the receptionist. I offered my business card and asked for my appointment. She looked at me and asked, "Are you Al Martin from Amelia?" I answered "Why, yes, I am." She said, "I'm Lucille." The spark was gone.

Chapter 32:

LITTLE BETTY ANN AND THE LONESOME CALL OF THE WHIP-POOR-WILL

After giving life to four boys, one can only imagine how my parents felt when their little girl came into their lives. The baby girl with those big, beautiful blue eyes and fine blond hair and sweet smile was such a blessing. Betty Ann was a bright light on that cold snowy December morning. Of course, they fell in love with her on sight, but as she developed her sweet personality, she was even more delightful to her parents, brothers, and all who knew her. She came along at a critical time in the lives of her parents in 1931, when they were feeling the depths of the Great Depression. They needed all the joy they could possibly get, and little Betty Ann gave it in abundance. Her mother so enjoyed washing and combing her long blonde hair, never having cut it. Even with the hard times they were having, their wonderful daughter brightened their lives beyond compare.

When Little Betty Ann was just twenty months old, a childhood disease struck, and in a short time she breathed her last breath. Their wonderful bright light was no more. To say they were devastated would be a great understatement. Their lives were torn apart, and for a time they had not wanted to live. Their world was shattered, but they realized they could not stop living. They had to go on. Their four sons depended on them. They prayed until their knees were sore. God brought them through, and they would go on, but would never forget their little Betty Ann. It was only their deep faith in God and in their personal Lord and Savior, Jesus, that they withstood their extreme grief in their loss and were able to go on with life.

My single most memorable time with my mother was while we were sitting on the back porch and hearing the call of the whip-poor-will down in the back field. I turned to her, and she had tears in her eyes and running down her cheeks. I asked what was wrong, and she told me perhaps the saddest yet sweetest story I've ever heard. She told me how Betty Ann, loved the sound of the whip-poor-will and how she would tilt her head with her blond ringlets and point to the sound that she loved so much. Mom told me how devastating the death of her only daughter had been, and still was, and how the call of the whip-poor-will would always be a lonesome call to her after Betty Ann's death. Mom's tears affirm to me that the love of a mother for a child is unending, and the mere passage of time cannot diminish that love. Although too young at the time to comprehend, I can now understand as tears well up in my own eyes as I relate that wonderful but sad story. I know my mother is now in heaven. I also know that she is with Betty Ann.

After my mother passed on, an old, yellowed sheet of paper was found among her belongings. Written by our cousin Vadie, these touching words describe the untimely death of Betty Ann.

"The death angel visited the home of Mr. and Mrs. Ruff Martin on September 7, 1934 and called their sweet child, Betty Ann, to her home above. Little Betty Ann was twenty months old, was a bright child and the only girl they had and all loved her, so it was hard to give her up. All was done that loving hands could do, yet she must go. Jesus said, "Suffer the little children to come unto me, for of such is the kingdom of Heaven." She was laid to rest in Little Flock Cemetery. She leaves to mourn a father, mother, four brothers and a host of relatives and friends. Little Betty Ann was like a blooming flower to soon fade away. We believe our loss is her eternal gain. On the Sunday following her passing, Elder J.M. Dickerson, conducted a funeral service and spoke many comforting words to the sorrowing ones."

Writing by Yavada Smith, Amelia, VA

Betty Ann was born and died before I was born, so I never knew her, but I have absolutely no doubt that I will know her in heaven. She will have beautiful blue eyes, long blond hair, and a sweet smile, and she will call out to me, for the first time ever. Along with her will be a beautiful older lady smiling who will say to me, "Hello, Alton, it's so good to see you." My mom, with her beautiful baby girl, perhaps listening to the call of the whip-poor-will and we can all listen together. Lonesome call no more.

Chapter 33:
MARTIN REUNIONS
AT LITTLE FLOCK

As previously mentioned, my dad had fifteen siblings, and several relocated to Amelia County, Virginia. I had the good fortune to grow up with several cousins, and they all attended Little Flock Church some of the time. This meant every Sunday at church was kind of like a Martin reunion. Many uncles and aunts were there to watch over us children. In addition to regular church services we always had our Martin reunions there on the grounds or later in the new basement. Of course, food was always a big part of these gatherings, in which I was always happy to participate. I sometimes think that when food is prepared by all the ladies in attendance, there is a little competition going on for the best dish. This is certainly to the benefit of connoisseurs of good food, like me, and I always felt obligated to sample all the dishes. Well, they did go to great trouble to prepare these delicious foods.

I don't know if it was the food or friendships that caused such crowds, but it seemed that there were always more Martins there than I knew about. Some of the Martins that still lived in Patrick would come to our reunions occasionally. Also, longtime friends came to make it even better. When I was young, people who didn't know me were introduced to me by my mom, saying, "This is Alton Ray, my baby boy." At that time, I didn't like the baby part, but later, as I grew up, I'd introduce myself as Rosie's baby boy. I don't remember her name or if she was a relative, but one older lady used to seek out all the younger boys to pat us on the face and kiss us. After a while I would be on the lookout for her and try to avoid her. She was relentless and would usually catch us by surprise, and when she did, the patting and kissing started. Oh well, it made her happy and I was never seriously injured by her attention.

After I moved away, my oldest brother George came back to live in Amelia, and everyone knew him but as time passed, some people were not exactly sure of my place in the line of Ruff and Rosie's boys. They would study my face and ask, "Which one are you?" I would obligingly say, "I'm Alton, the baby." That problem, and in an effort to get a little levity in these gatherings, caused me to come up with an idea for the next reunion. Actually, things could get a little boring after a couple hours. So, for the next reunion I made a name tag of sorts, which read, "Hello, cousin. I'm Alton Ray, Ruff and Rosie's baby boy and George's brother". This caused a few smiles and some additional talk. Mission accomplished.

Now that all the uncles and aunts have all passed on, all the relatives are cousins, and many I haven't even met, and others I don't recognize. I recently attended the funeral services at Little Flock of a 100-year-old cousin. As I stepped into the church, I was surprised at the small number of people there but began to think about her age and the fact that most all her peers likely had already passed on. That would explain the low numbers. Then, as I looked around I recognized absolutely no one. I began to think that I was at the wrong funeral or at the wrong time. Everyone was gray headed like me, and old like me. I struck up a conversation with a man who I found out was, guess what, my cousin. He introduced me to his mother who, of course, was even older. She said to me, "Sit down here and talk to me". I did as directed. I don't know how old she was, but she was a delightful person and made my trip worthwhile. I asked her son if he knew if the daughter of the deceased was in attendance. He did, and she was, and he directed me to the front pew. I looked up there and found a bunch of old folks. They were all gray headed and old. How could that be? She was my peer. The daughter, Brenda jumped up and greeted me with great exuberance, and I enjoyed our visit. There is just something about an old person's funeral that makes it just like family reunions. I had a good time at my 100-year-old cousin's going away party. I think from now on I'll try to look at funerals as a true celebration, not sadly but happily, because that is not the end but the beginning. God and His son Jesus made great plans for His own. I'm sure my cousin is having a constant reunion with all our uncles, aunts, cousins, my siblings and my parents. What a day that will be. That's the big reunion.

My advice to you is if your family is not having reunions, start one soon. Also, if you haven't prepared for the big one, start now.

While our parents were alive, there was always a wonderful sense of home at their house, no matter what day or time. We were always welcome there, even if we woke them in the middle of the night. I'd been there often and at odd times and was always welcomed with open arms. Usually, I was asked if I was hungry. After our parents died, we brothers decided that we should start our own brothers' reunions. We knew this would be pleasing to Dad and Mom because they always loved to see the boys get together. Also, we thought that we'd most likely not get together unless we made plans, since some of us lived in different states. George, Bob and I lived in Virginia, Marion lived in North Carolina, Lee in Florida, and Don in Tennessee. Over the years, we had four reunions in Virginia, three in North Carolina, and two in Tennessee. We met in various places, such as a Methodist retreat, motels, homes and a Chickahominy River log cabin. They were all wonderful, and the talk ranged from our lives at home with our parents to our current lives. I noticed there was a lot of conversation about where we would be eating. At breakfast, we talked about where we'd be for lunch, and at lunch about where we would eat dinner, and then back to breakfast. Some things never change.

The first two reunions were with just the boys in attendance, but we missed our wives, so we invited them from then on. They added to the conversation and to our pleasure. A few times, we stayed where we could cook our own food, and the ladies sure helped the quality of food and talk.

I heard that all good things must eventually end, so our reunions have ended. All my brothers have passed on to that great reunion in heaven. I'll join them later.

Chapter 34:
LITTLE FLOCK CHURCH

Little Flock Primitive Baptist Church, the church of my childhood, stood in a grove of heart pine trees in the "Little Patrick" section of Amelia County. Most of the people there had either moved from Patrick County or were, like me, children of people who had moved from Patrick County. Many were my aunts and uncles or cousins. Everyone knew everyone and all about everyone. As I write this, I can see them all and am reminded of the hymn "Precious Memories" how they flood my soul. All the hymns were sung with no musical accompaniment and, most of the time, led by my Dad's brother, my Uncle Joe. When he started a song and it didn't go well, he stopped and started over. He knew all the hymns and how to sing them, and if you didn't sing as he wanted, he'd start again, with or without anyone else.

Uncle Joe was somewhat of a character and possibly adding to his persona was his missing eye. When he was much younger back on his father's farm, Uncle Joe made the mistake of getting behind an especially cantankerous mule, which is not unusual for mules. This one was feeling especially out of sorts, and he just hauled off and kicked Uncle Joe in the eye. The eye was lost, so someone sewed the eye lids together and that was how old Uncle Joe looked for the rest of his life. One might think that Uncle Joe would be cantankerous too, after losing an eye, but he was one of the nicest guys around and a real asset to Little Flock Church.

At the time of my childhood, Little Flock Church had a traveling minister who came from North Carolina to Little Flock Church each second

Sunday. Although he didn't officially get paid, I remember seeing men shaking hands with him and leaving a five-dollar bill in his hand. The Primitive Baptist preachers were men full of the Spirit, with no seminary education. They had other jobs, and gave of themselves to the church, simply to serve the Lord and His people, without pay.

The church building was frame built and with white clapboard siding. It had one big room that was the sanctuary with straight backed pews and hard seats. There was a raised platform for the choir and podium for the preacher. The building had no electricity until years after the building was built. A potbellied stove was up near the front. Out back behind the church were two outhouses, each with two seats for no waiting. I remember an upgrade that was made to real toilet paper in place of Sears, Roebuck paper. High living indeed.

On the left side of the church were tall pine trees with plank tables attached. The tables were laden with some of the best country cooking at least once a year. There was finger-licking fried chicken, pork, beef, all kinds of good vegetables, pies, cakes, and other goodies that would tempt a saint. The only problem was that the food was always under tablecloths to keep the flies away and would not be uncovered until all the people came out of church. This seemed like an eternity, and, of course, being a good boy, I never touched anything unless no one was looking, until the preacher gave an unending blessing. The wait was well worth it.

The cemetery was over on the right side of the church. I've been to many of the funerals conducted at Little Flock and many of the people there in the cemetery are relatives of mine: My father and mother, my mother's father and stepmother are there, my brother George and his wife, Arlene, and their son, Billy, my sister Betty Ann, my brother Bob, his wife, Jean and innumerable uncles, aunts, cousins, and many family friends. Headstones will read: Martin, Mills, Smith, Burcham, all relatives of mine. My brother Don has a stone there but is buried in Caracas, Venezuela, where he had a fatal accident.

Most of my memories are on the inside of the church with preaching going on, it seemed, all day. Sometimes, there would be more than one preacher and each one wanted to have his time to "say a few words." Some sermons had few words, and some had more, but to a young boy they all seemed to have way too many. The ladies of the church were usually up close to the platform in the "Amen" section, and the men, many dressed in bib overhauls, were in the back, closer to the door, for quicker escape, I guess. Some slept and others fidgeted, others paid attention. I was usually in the "fidgeted" section or outside with some other boys, looking at the old Model A's, Model T's, or other cars and trucks. In the summertime, if I was inside, I was watching the wasps come in through the open windows, circling the big rods that went from side to side, holding the walls together. Sometimes, women would nurse their babies without modesty, so I watched in amazement as they exposed their full breasts.

Some years later, that building was torn down and a new brick building with modern facilities, such as heating and air conditioning, and actual indoor restrooms, were added along with real toilet paper. No more outhouses.

Baptizing in the River

Little Flock was a fundamental Baptist church, and they believed in fundamental things such as baptizing in the river, creek, or pond. I still see that as a very moving and spiritual way to baptize and have seen this in my adult life as well. Although I have never seen a wintertime baptizing, I have been told that they are still done outside, even if there is ice in the water, and no one has gotten sick because of it. I think God approves. Jesus said to accept Him and be baptized. As a very young boy, I remember my mother being baptized in a mill pond, and I did not understand what was happening and was very upset. She comforted me afterwards.

Foot Washing

Another practice at Little Flock was foot washing. This is biblical, as in the book of John, chapter 13, verses 5-8, when Jesus washed the feet of the disciples. They did this at Little Flock, even though I never saw this, but have participated in it elsewhere. I believe this indicates an act of service to others and shows humility. Jesus was God in the flesh, so He surely did not need to be humble, but He showed us how to be humble.

I know that the people who went to Little Flock were wonderful people. My memories of the church and its people are vivid and fond.

God's Plan of Salvation

The most wonderful thing I've ever learned in Church has been about God's plan of salvation, or how to get to Heaven after our earthly life is over. Some may think that being good is the way to Heaven, however, that's not what the Bible teaches. In fact, the Bible says that you can't get to Heaven by your good works, but only through the grace of God. It's not even going to church on a regular basis, but only through God's son, Jesus. It is recorded in the book of John, Chapter 14, verse 6, Jesus said, "I am the way and the truth and the life. No one comes to the Father except through me."